Group Techniques

Group Techniques

Gerald Corey *California State University, Fullerton*

Marianne Schneider Corey *Private Practice*

Patrick J. Callanan *Private Practice*

J. Michael Russell *California State University, Fullerton*

Brooks/Cole Publishing Company
Monterey, California

Brooks/Cole Publishing Company
A Division of Wadsworth, Inc.

Printed in the United States of America
10 9 8 7 6 5 4

Library of Congress Cataloging in Publication Data:

Main entry under title:

Group techniques.

  Bibliography: p.
  Includes index.
  1. Group relations training.   I. Corey,
Gerald F.
HM134.G748   158'.3   81-38535
ISBN 0-8185-0472-2   AACR2

Subject Editor: *Claire L. Verduin*
Manuscript Editor: *Pamela Fischer*
Production Editors: *Jennifer Young/Micky Lawler*
Interior & Cover Design: *Jamie Sue Brooks*
Typesetting: *Graphic Typesetting Service, Los Angeles, California*

This book is dedicated to
the teachers who gave us the benefit of their wisdom
and to our group members,
especially those in our residential workshops,
who gave us the opportunity to learn more.

Preface

Since the four of us began working together in 1972, we have been involved in almost every aspect of group work—as members, leaders, teachers, and workshop conductors. In the course of this long involvement we have found ourselves continually faced with questions about techniques in groups: their place, their usefulness, their abuse. In many of our training workshops we have observed beginning leaders flounder in their use of techniques. In professional workshops we have been asked about techniques in such a fashion as to imply that there is or should be a scientific body of techniques available to the practitioner to cover every eventuality in a group.

Our primary assumption in this book is that techniques are never the main course in group work. This assumption has many implications. It puts the focus on the members and the leader and on what goes on between them. Whatever obscures these relationships is not facilitative in our minds. Thus techniques are means, not ends; they are not to be hidden behind, are not to be forced on the client; they should be used to increase knowledge and awareness. They are fundamentally at the service of the client, not the therapist.

To avoid having the techniques described in this book used as the primary focus of group work, we do not attempt to provide an exhaustive catalog of techniques and exercises. Our purpose is not to outline all possible techniques for every possible population, but to teach leaders how to develop and use techniques in group work. You can best use this book by reading a chapter, putting the book down, and then asking yourself what relevance the techniques described have for you in your situation and how they might be applied. We hope you will not borrow our techniques verbatim and use them without consideration for the members of your groups and their unique relationships with you and with each other.

In addition to our hopes for the way this book will be used, we also hope that it will stimulate your interest in the broad field of working with people in groups and in the philosophical and ethical dimensions of what you do. Such an interest could lead you to think about theories of therapy, to further your own therapy, to engage in exchanges of ideas rather than being professionally isolated, and to participate in professional workshops. It could also lead you to an interest in supervision, whether in the formal sense of teaching or in the informal sense of working with a respected colleague. If this book motivates you and other practitioners and students to broaden your interest to encompass the whole field of counseling and therapy, we believe that interest will help to diminish the abuse of techniques.

We sought to write this book in a style that fits our personal perspective and our way of leading groups. We have not included references to other authors within the body of the text. We hope you will use the selected bibliography at the end of the book to further your thinking about group work. We do not want to give the impression, however, that the techniques discussed arose in a vacuum. In addition to being direct responses to problems presented by participants in groups we have led, the techniques in this book bear the stamp of our own therapists, of leaders of groups and workshops in which we have been members, and of a great many writers with various theoretical orientations.

This book is for students and practitioners in any human-services field, from counseling psychology to social work, where group is an accepted modality. In the classroom it can be a valuable auxiliary text. In practice it can be used to stimulate thinking and creativity in one's approach to group work, and it can be used in conjunction with supervision. Intended readers include psychiatric nurses, social workers, psychologists, ministers, marriage and family therapists, teachers, and mental health professionals and paraprofessionals who lead groups.

We would like to thank those who read the manuscript in its developmental stages and who offered suggestions for improving the book, including Jeffrey A. Kottler, University of North Alabama; Al'an Dye, Purdue University; Jerrold Shapiro, King Kalakaua Center for Humanistic Psychotherapy and University of Hawaii; Mary Moline, Loma Linda University; Beverly Palmer, California State University, Dominguez

Hills; and Donna Robbins. Several students also gave us valuable comments as they used the manuscript in their group-leadership class: Linda Boehm Callanan, Alisa Engel, Matthew Hamlin, Chris Boyd, Deborah Douglas, Gary Charleston, and Sandie Jacobs. We extend our special thanks to our manuscript editor, Pam Fischer, whose editorial expertise helped the four of us to achieve a unified style.

Gerald Corey
Marianne Schneider Corey
Patrick J. Callanan
J. Michael Russell

Contents

CHAPTER **3 Techniques for Preparing Groups** 33

CHAPTER **4 Techniques for the Initial and Transition Stages** 56

CHAPTER **5 Techniques for the Working Stage** 90

The Authors

 **I am Gerald Corey**, currently a professor of human services at California State University at Fullerton. I teach courses in counseling theory and practice, group counseling, and group process. I am also a licensed psychologist in California and a diplomate in counseling psychology, American Board of Professional Psychology. I received my doctorate in counseling from the University of Southern California in 1967. I have worked as a counseling psychologist in two universities, and have taught at several universities and colleges and a high school.

Recently, I've been teaching graduate courses and offering workshops in group counseling in England, Germany, and Mexico, as well as in the United States. It is exciting and challenging to me to work with professionals who have a variety of backgrounds and interests. Not only have I learned about the practical applications of group techniques from those who have participated in my workshops, but I've also come increasingly to appreciate the value of group work with many different populations. Along with Marianne and Mike, I conducted a weeklong personal-growth group in Germany and another weeklong training and supervision group for counselors in the U.S. Army drug and alcohol rehabilitation program. Along with Marianne and Patrick, I regularly offer in-service training workshops for group workers at a state facility for the rehabilitation of sex offenders. And, with Patrick, Mike, and Marianne, I look forward to the weeklong residential personal-growth groups we offer in Idyllwild, California each summer.

Working with Mike, Marianne, and Patrick on this book has been fun as well as work. They do their best to challenge me and keep me honest, and I continue to value the personal relationship that enhances our professional relationship. This book is an outgrowth of the time we have spent together and of the various workshops we've led as a team.

My preferred modality for therapeutic work is groups. Groups provide an outlet for creative expression as well as an opportunity to work with my friends and colleagues. My experiences as a client in groups have been significant in my development.

Because I work hard, I realize the necessity of recreation. I find walking in the mountains, bicycling, and traveling truly replenishing. Attending professional conferences and conventions and meeting with professionals who share similar interests is a source of renewal for both Marianne and myself. Talking with my two teenage daughters, Heidi and Cindy, continues to be a nourishing experience.

Fortunately, I find a great deal of meaning in my work as a professor, a consultant, a practitioner, and an author. I have found that writing textbooks is a natural extension of working closely with students as a teacher. I have authored or co-authored the following books, all of which have been published by Brooks/Cole: *Theory and Practice of Counseling and Psychotherapy*, Second Edition (and *Manual*) (1982), *Case Approach to Counseling and Psychotherapy* (1982), *Theory and Practice of Group Counseling* (and *Manual*) (1981), *Professional and Ethical Issues in Counseling and Psychotherapy* (1979, with Marianne Schneider Corey and Patrick J. Callanan), *I Never Knew I Had a Choice* (1978, with Marianne Schneider Corey), and *Groups: Process and Practice (1977, with Marianne Schneider Corey).*

I am Marianne Schneider Corey, a licensed marriage, family, and child therapist in California. I am in private practice, doing individual and group counseling. I regularly lead training workshops for professional staff at a state hospital and for students in human services at California State University at Fullerton. In addition, I have conducted with Jerry and Mike a training workshop near my home town in Germany for German and American counselors. I am also involved in coleading couples' groups and weeklong residential groups. Over the past ten years, I have worked with the elderly, adolescents, children, and institutionalized persons. My present practice involves working with a relatively well-functioning, middle-aged population. Jerry and I are the current chairpersons of the Professional Standards and Ethics Committee of the Association for Specialists in Group Work, and along with Jerry and Patrick I am writing *Casebook on Ethical Standards for Group Counseling and Psychotherapy* for that association. I have co-authored *I Never Knew I Had a Choice* (1978, with Gerald Corey), *Groups: Process and Practice* (1977, with Gerald Corey), and *Professional and Ethical Issues in Counseling and Psychotherapy* (1977, with Gerald Corey and Patrick J. Callanan). My preference is group work. I see it as the most effective format in which to work with clients and the most rewarding for me personally.

I believe that my education and training as a therapist are never finished. I attend workshops for personal and professional growth. I am an avid reader and seek to keep an open mind about many different aspects of life. My education and personal therapy, my colleagues and friends have been important in my development as a therapist. In addition, many of the ways I approach clients and counseling are the result of my values and my upbringing in a small country village in Germany. I married Jerry 17 years ago, and we have two children. I struggle to effectively combine my role as a parent and my role as a therapist. I see my nuclear and extended family as my primary group.

The writing of this book has been exciting, fun, and rewarding. It has given me the opportunity to share my enthusiasm and ideas about group techniques. I have been forced to examine and question my ideas before putting them on paper. I have spent many hours with my co-authors, who are my good friends and colleagues. While undertaking a serious task, we have had many good times together and have enjoyed the project immensely.

I am Patrick J. Callanan, a licensed marriage, family, and child therapist in California. I maintain a private practice in the Santa Ana and Tustin areas of Orange County. My first contact with formal therapy was in a group in the fall of 1971. I have been associated with group therapy, in one form or another, ever since; it is my modality of choice. Each year I participate as a leader in a weeklong residential workshop through California State University at Fullerton. I have been a panel member at professional conventions and workshops. I conduct training workshops for professional staff at a state hospital and for students in human services at California State University at Fullerton. With the Coreys I have co-authored *Professional and Ethical Issues in Counseling and Psychotherapy* (1979), and also with the Coreys I am writing *Casebook on Ethical Standards for Group Counseling and Psychotherapy* for the Association for Specialists in Group Work. All these experiences challenge my thinking and influence my behavior both as a person and as a professional. The most rewarding of my experiences have been the many conversations, discussions, arguments with my friends and colleagues, including particularly my co-authors in this project.

I am deeply committed to my work and to learning all that I can about doing it effectively. This I see as an unfinishable task; there is always something new to learn. My contributions to this book are based on what I was taught and what I have observed. I pass it on and continue to learn and observe. I am grateful for the friends and colleagues who were sent my way and delighted with myself for pursuing a relationship with them.

I am J. Michael Russell, a professor of human services and professor of philosophy at California State University at Fullerton. In my doctoral dissertation in philosophy (University of California at Santa Barbara, 1971) and in my subsequent research I have sought to blend an exploration of philosophical psychology with a concern about concrete existential struggles. I have published articles on "Psychotherapy and Quasi-Performative Speech" *(Behaviorism,* 1973), "Saying, Feeling, and Self-Deception" *(Behaviorism,* 1979), "Sartre, Therapy, and Expanding the Concept of Responsibility" *(American Journal of Psychoanalysis,* 1979), "Sartre's Theory of Sexuality" *(Journal of Humanistic Psychology,* 1979), "How to Think about Thinking" *(Journal of Mind and Behavior,* 1980), "A Weeklong Residential Workshop" *(Journal of Specialists in Group Work,* 1980), and "Reflection and Self-Deception" *(Research in Phenomenology,* 1981). I have been involved in leading personal-growth workshops and teaching personal-growth courses since 1971 and have presented numerous lectures, papers, and panel discussions on group work to various professional organizations of psychologists and counselors. The existentialist philosopher Sartre has had the greatest impact on my thinking, but I have also been very much influenced by Freud and by Fritz Perls.

Jerry and Marianne Corey, Patrick Callanan, and I have been lecturing together, coleading groups, and having an impact on one another's lives since 1972, and that interaction has been enormously fulfilling for me. Most of this book was written as the four of us collaborated around a table in the Corey home, and, solely on the grounds that I was the fastest typist, it typically fell to me to piece together what we each had to say. It was a joy to discover how often we spoke as if with one voice.

Group Techniques

CHAPTER ONE

The Role of Techniques

At the outset, we need to be clear about what we mean by the word *technique*. This task is not as easy as it may sound. How does one look at the therapeutic journey and decide which parts of it can be described as techniques and which parts belong to the person of the counselor? Freud's couch is surely a technique as is free association. But were Freud's position behind the couch and the manner in which he spoke with his patients techniques? Is Carl Rogers's warm, empathetic style a technique? Is his selective reflection of a client's utterances a technique? Was Fritz Perls's demeanor a technique? One could answer yes to all these questions and in a sense we do. Virtually anything a leader does can be viewed as a technique, including being silent, maintaining eye contact, arranging seating, and presenting interpretations.

Because it would be difficult to write a book with such a broad conception, we generally use the term *technique* to refer to cases where the leader makes an explicit and directive request of a member for the purpose of focusing on material, augmenting or exaggerating affect, practicing behavior, or solidifying insight. This definition encompasses, for instance, the following procedures: conducting initial interviews in which members are asked to focus on their reasons for wanting to join a group, asking a nonproductive group to clarify the direction it wants to take, asking a member to role-play a specific situation, asking a member to practice a behavior, encouraging a person to repeat certain words or to complete a sentence, helping members summarize what they got out of a group session, challenging a member's belief system, and working with the cognitions of a member that influence behavior. We also

1

consider as techniques procedures aimed at helping group leaders get focused for group sessions—techniques leaders can use to give them a sense of the direction they might pursue with a group.

Avoiding the misuse of techniques

Misconceptions about the use of techniques abound. When we give workshops about groups, participants often ask for techniques for working with specific clients. The implication seems to be that to lead a group effectively one should have the "right" technical tools to employ at the "right" moment, as if there were a precise scientific procedure for each and every situation and as if such procedures were all that needed to be imparted in a training session. We think this attitude indicates an unwillingness to learn about how groups evolve and function. Perhaps for some models of group counseling, such as behavior modification, specific methods are appropriate to secure well-defined behavioral outcomes. However, although the people who attend our workshops are apparently, like us, more interested in insight therapy than in behavior modification, they nevertheless seem eager to obtain gimmicks and quick solutions—short cuts that protect them from full involvement with their groups.

Given our assumption that techniques are means and not ends, we naturally have some concerns about how this book will be used: Will the book contribute to the problem of group leaders being too technique oriented? Will readers memorize specific devices and use them insensitively, rather than treating the book as a means to deepen their own therapeutic inventiveness and judgment? We would like instead to inspire leaders' own creativity, to have the book be a jumping-off place that encourages leaders to take risks in trying out and spontaneously inventing techniques.

It is impossible to predict, except in a general way, what the nature of a group will be. Thus a recipe-book approach to therapy and techniques, while providing opportunities to try different things, surely does not replace the main function of a group leader. The analogy to recipes and cooking is helpful here. Many an excellent cook—and this would be our recommendation for the therapist—creates a different dish each time: even though working from a basic recipe, one has to follow one's taste, use foods available at the market that day, and trust one's own sensitivity.

Paying attention to the obvious.   It is our assumption that techniques can further and deepen feelings that are already present and that they should preferably grow out of what is already taking place. When a person says "I'm feeling lonely," for example, it is appropriate to introduce a technique to help move this feeling further. For this reason, we generally prefer to include the members in the selection of group themes rather than to arbitrarily select a theme. This is not a hard and fast rule; many group practitioners work effectively with preselected techniques, exercises, and themes. Indeed, for certain populations, this approach is indicated. We sometimes use techniques to initiate material at the beginning of a group and often use them to summarize material at the end. But generally we use techniques for elaborating on what is already present. We are distrustful of having too much of a preset agenda for group process; we prefer to take our clues from what the members provide.

Many groups have moments of stagnation, periods of resistance or hesitation. It is easy in these situations—and often quite unwise—to hasten to employ a technique to get things moving rather than to pay attention to the important material being presented. Seeming lack of movement is important in itself, and anxiety should not lead therapists to introduce a gimmick in order to avoid a period in which nothing seems to be happening. By looking around the room, for example, you may notice that members are disengaged—they appear bored, they are fidgeting, they are falling asleep. We think the best technique at such times is for you to initiate a check-out process: "I'm aware of working hard to bring some life to this group, and I'm aware that many of you don't appear involved in what's going on. I'd like to find out from each of you what is happening." You can then share your feelings at the moment or you can save them until the members have expressed what they are feeling. What we see as a mistake is to try technique after technique to generate movement in a situation such as this. We'd prefer to deal with what is actually occurring within the group.

In addition, when considering whether to introduce a technique, you should take into account the stage the group is in. For instance, you can expect trust to be an issue in the initial stages of a group. A group may be somewhat silent and cautious at this point in its existence. To introduce a technique to get things moving is to ignore the obvious and to impose a dynamic that is either premature for the group or alien to the character of the group. Doing so radically interferes with the natural development of the group. By introducing instead a technique that stresses and clarifies what is happening, you augment rather than intrude on the process. Then the technique completes the process and does not ignore it.

Maintaining flexibility.   Just as leaders should not be rigid about which material to work with, they should not be rigid about where a technique is supposed to go. As a leader, you must be ready to flow wherever the material may lead. You must be prepared to abandon a technique that seems to lead nowhere or to modify it as needed. We once witnessed a therapist demonstrating work with an angry woman; he kept urging her to hit a pillow with her hands, apparently failing to notice or being too rigid to adjust to the fact that she was already strangling it. We wished that he had been aware of and ready to work with the material she was presenting. To take a different illustration, a leader may determine that a client needs to pursue an issue with her father. The leader may introduce a technique designed to accentuate her sadness and yet should be ready to work with the client's showing anger instead. In a group therapy session we supervised, a violent patient kept reiterating that he was "different." The leader insisted on this client's dealing with his violent feelings rather than exploring his more pressing concern about being different. The leader had already decided that the work was going to be on anger and was not ready to flow with material more ready to be pursued. Either theme could have been worked with, but it seemed to us that the session did not progress as much as it might have because of the therapist's inflexibility.

However, although it is possible to make mistakes because of insensitivity to promising and pressing material, we would not want leaders to become too anxious about pursuing the "right" or the "most pressing" material. Often several directions are equally worth pursuing with a client. When we have been asked why we chose one direction rather than another in a given situation, we often have felt that, although we had our reasons for what we did, it would not have been wrong to take a quite different direction for different and valid reasons. Here the group leader's own interests and level of energy should and do come into play.

The therapeutic relationship

Much of the opportunity for significant change in clients is based on their relationship with the group leader. Just as many of the behaviors we label maladaptive had their origins in early faulty relationships, so too new behaviors can be cemented through the new relationship with the leader. If this relationship is inauthentic, superficial, or otherwise impoverished, we doubt that clients will make significant strides in making desired changes. Change makes too many demands on a person to be accomplished through the use of techniques alone. Change must be tested and tried out, and the therapeutic relationship provides this testing ground. Let's look at two issues in the use of techniques that illustrate the significance of the therapeutic relationship.

Timing the use of techniques.   A critical factor in group work is that techniques be used with consideration for the readiness of clients to give up defenses. To push beyond a client's readiness to move is to violate the client's integrity. To assault defenses without consideration for their importance in maintaining equilibrium is to expose a client to possibly serious psychological damage. No technique will provide you with information on how ready clients are to give up their defenses. This knowledge requires delicacy and a sensitivity to the client's present state of mind. You need intelligence, wisdom, and above all a concerned attentiveness to your relationship with your clients. This relationship provides clients with the hold on reality that is needed to make the move away from nonproductive and excessively defensive conduct. As group members learn to trust and believe in you, they are likely to move toward personal freedom. In the absence of such a relationship, clients are asked to trust techniques without any sign of your concern for them. Clients in that position do well to resist. If clients lack the ego strength to resist, they are prodded along by techniques alone, with little support from you as a caring person. The therapist who pays attention to the leader/client relationship develops a sixth sense that makes it possible to gauge the course of therapy and to judge the optimum time for gently pushing the client into areas previously avoided. This skill is above and beyond technique. In some fashion it is a part of the therapist from the beginning, but it can be refined to a great degree through training and supervision.

Avoiding self-deception in using techniques.   Techniques can be powerful sources for emotional release and can generate tremendous energy in the therapeutic group. But they can easily mask the relationship between the leader and the member. When the storm has subsided, any insights gained can be easily dismissed by the client as having been brought about by something foreign to the client's own resources: the power of a special environment or the magic of the leader's technical skills. At the other extreme, because of the impact of a cathartic moment, a client can cling to the false belief that the issue has now been worked on and is finished. Catharsis can be exciting, and yet it can feed a false sense of productivity. The leader who is too hungry to produce a heavy emotional session may use techniques to generate the appearance of movement without being sensitive to the need to work the material through and to gain some comprehension of its meanings and implications.

Choosing techniques

Several different techniques can often be used in the same situation, and each may be equally beneficial to a client. What basis does a leader have for choosing one technique rather than another?

Theory as a basis.   The theoretical persuasion of the group leader often dictates the selection of a technique. For example, free association with minimal intrusion from the leader usually leads to regression. A hot-chair technique focuses a client on the here-and-now. A technique of reflection and acceptance from the therapist places the emphasis on the client, not on the therapist. Techniques of reinforcement for behavior focus attention on behavior, not on intrapersonal dynamics. Consistent emphasis on the consequences of behavior eventually focuses clients on reality. Thus, the choice of techniques depends to some extent on the theoretical framework of the therapist.

Population as a basis.   We believe that a sensitivity to the population you are dealing with should be manifest in the kinds of techniques you choose to use. One cannot use the same kinds of techniques with a group of organic-brain-syndrome patients in a hospital as with clients in a growth group. Likewise, techniques that tend to bring strong emotions to the surface need to be used cautiously with a group for the criminally insane when violent emotional outbursts are the presenting problem. Techniques used for group therapy clients may be inappropriate for professionals such as nurses or teachers in an interpersonal-skills-development group. We cannot describe the almost limitless variation in groups in purpose, age, and level of functioning. We do say that a leader needs constantly to ask "Is this technique fitted and suitable for this group of people? Is it the best available technique for this population in this situation?"

Personality as a basis.   A technique should also be chosen with consideration for the personality of the individual client. If it does not fit, then it does not facilitate the genuine meeting of human beings. For example, imagine asking a reserved, middle-aged, upper-class woman to use four-letter, abrasive words as an expression of her anger. Although the therapist may feel it valuable for her to express anger, it is equally important to respect her sensitivity to such language. There must be a congruence of the technique, the person introducing it, and the person for whom it is intended.

Introducing techniques

We think it is important for you to pay attention to how you introduce techniques. To what extent do you explain them? How do you ask members to participate in them? How do you work with members who are reluctant to follow your suggestions?

Explaining techniques.   You can't always explain to a client in detail what the proposed technique is, the rationale for its use, and the desired outcome. To do so may render the technique useless. For instance, a lengthy explanation may interrupt the flow of the material. Or an explanation that specifies an anticipated emotion—"You'll probably experience a lot of pain and cry if you do this"—may set the client up to artificially display that feeling or to talk about it. In our groups we also do not usually explain the outcome exactly because we ourselves are not always sure what may develop. For example, a woman says she feels she may be too critical, and so we introduce an exercise that encourages her to be critical based on our hunch that being critical is indeed a part of her; we suspect the outcome, but we leave it to the process to prove whether our hunch is correct. We do not mean to imply that everything about techniques has to be mysterious. Part of the preparation of group members should include discussion about techniques and how they serve the purpose of a group. In our groups we discuss the limitations we place on ourselves—how far we are willing to go in the use of techniques. We sometimes mention the experiences we have had with techniques in our personal therapy. This kind of explanation does little to make techniques ineffective and may greatly lessen clients' fears of them.

Inviting members to participate.   It is our practice to invite group members to go along with a technique and to proceed only when we sense that we have their permission. We tend to use such phrases as "Are you willing to take this further?" "Are you willing to try this?" "I have something in mind that might help you understand better what you are saying. Let me tell you what it is, and see whether you are willing to go along with it."

Working with reluctance on the part of clients.   If the client says that he or she is not willing, we then might say "Are you willing to talk about why you hesitate?" If the answer is still negative, we usually let it go. But we keep the incident in mind, and if at a later point the client speaks of how little he or she is getting from the group we then point out how unwilling he or she has been to risk doing something different. We justify this position on the basis that, on the one hand, clients should not be harassed or pushed into doing what they are unwilling to do, but, on the other hand, a group often needs to exert some pressure for many clients to get work done.

Note that we request our clients to talk about why they do not want to go along with a technique. This is a genuine request, and we do not automatically label their behavior resistance. We think that a lot of "resistance" is justified caution on the part of the client. Most often members are willing to talk about their reluctance, and almost inevitably this discussion leads to important issues for the group, such as the trust or distrust felt toward certain members or perhaps toward the leader. Hence, at this point, the sensitive leader abandons the technique, perhaps introducing a different technique appropriate for pursuing the theme of lack of trust. For example, the leader might now say "Perhaps, then, you would try this instead. Would you be willing to say to each person in this group—myself included—something about each of us that makes it easy or difficult for you to feel trust?" This technique can lead to good outcomes for the group, increased cohesion, and willingness in the future to go along with suggested techniques.

The person of the leader

We want to emphasize the leader's involvement in moving the group forward. In this regard, the character, the personal qualities, the philosophy of life of the leader are more important than any technique for facilitating the group process. You, as a group leader, are more than the sum total of your skills. From this viewpoint, when you take a technique that is not a reflection of your own character from another source—or even if you invent such a technique—you introduce something that is alien to you; it might more properly be regarded as a gimmick than as a technique, more of a trick than the basis for a genuine human encounter. For instance, if you are a low-key person and you introduce an aggressive technique, chances are that the discrepancy will inhibit the group. Imagine Fritz Perls sitting behind the couch with a notebook; B. F. Skinner saying "How does that make you feel?"; or Freud directing a patient to talk to an empty chair.

Too often those who lead groups look for techniques for every possible occurrence. They overrely on techniques to pull themselves out of difficult situations, to get groups moving or to keep them moving, and in doing so they become mechanical facilitators. They ignore the most powerful resources for reaching the members of their groups—their own reactions, their values, and the behavior they exhibit. We hope that you will acquire knowledge of how groups function, that you will learn the necessary skills and techniques to implement your knowledge in actual group work, and yet that you will do so in such a way that your techniques become an expression of your personal style and an extension of the unique person you are. We hope that you will take what we have to offer in these chapters and create your own variations—that you will develop a recipe that suits your taste. We are proposing an experimental attitude, and we encourage you to try out techniques and different ways of working in a group to gradually learn what works for you, as well as what does not.

How can you use techniques that are an extension of yourself as a person? We'd like to make some suggestions that will enhance your use of techniques and that will help you acquire techniques and a style that fit your personality.

Pay attention to yourself. A good place to begin is by paying attention to yourself. This self-examination includes looking at the impact you have on a group. It also includes assessing your level of investment, your directness, your willingness to model what you expect of your members, and your willingness to be psychologically present for them.

Learn to trust yourself. Learning to trust yourself is another essential part of the task of finding a style that suits your personality. If you do not trust your hunches, you may hold yourself back from even trying certain techniques. One way to develop this kind of trust is by being willing to follow your hunches and by trying variations of the techniques we describe. If a technique doesn't work, the consequences don't have to be horrible. Simply acknowledging that an exercise or a technique is not working is often the best way of pulling yourself out of a situation that could otherwise become worse. If you aren't willing to make some mistakes, if you are bound by being sure before you act, you miss many opportunities for action, and your clients are deprived of opportunities as well. We admit that what we advocate takes courage. It takes a willingness to risk making mistakes and to admit errors.

Model. Another way to be sure that your use of techniques reflects your personality is through modeling. Be aware of your thoughts and feelings as they surface within you in a group, and be willing to voice them. In so doing you communicate to your group that it is acceptable to have and to show feelings. You open the way for members to express themselves through your own modeling. For example, if you are feeling sad and express this sadness, your resulting ability and willingness to be touched by others who are sad, and to empathize with them can help them to fully explore the experience and the meaning of their sadness. Your behavior can be a catalyst in assisting those members to explore rather than to cut off their feelings. If you are not afraid of emotional intensity and if you keep in contact with members as they share deep feelings, then other members are likely to face and deal with their struggles. Modeling is not a technique to stir up feelings but an invitation to members to get in contact with their experience largely through the example of the leader. A potential danger here is that you may end up expressing your personal concerns more often than any member of the group. If you become aware of doing so, you need to ask yourself: "Am I using the group for self-indulgent purposes? Am I at a point where personal counseling for myself is indicated?" Your self-disclosures should be relevant to what is going on in the group, and the time you take should not be at the members' expense. Your disclosures should facilitate self-exploration and interaction within the group rather than burdening the members with your personal issues.

In addition to encouraging members to express their feelings, you can also influence members' behaviors through the process of modeling. You can invite members to broaden their range of in-group behavior by demonstrating certain behaviors yourself. You can teach directness through your own directness. You can encourage members to give sensitive and honest feedback to others by doing so yourself. If you model nonjudgmental confrontation in a way that shows your concern for the person being challenged, then your group members learn how to confront one another in the same fashion. Through your openness, members are invited to share what they are experiencing.

Approaching group sessions with a sense of enthusiasm generates enthusiasm within the group. Your enthusiasm and your being psychologically present for members are in themselves powerful modeling agents in getting groups to move. Your degree of aliveness and enthusiasm may be an index of the degree to which your groups are able to function in a vital way.

In summary, techniques have more impact if you are able to maintain a relationship with group members that is based on trust. Such trust is best created through the personal qualities that you project. In other words, techniques do not work in isolation from the leader's personality and relationship with members. Techniques are received in the light of the attitudes of the leaders who use them.

Concluding comments

The key point we have wanted to make in this chapter is that techniques are valuable and important but they must be used with caution. Because of the immediate progress techniques seem to promote, the therapist may draw on them rigidly and mechanically or leave unexplored material that they bring out. Techniques should be generated in and for the situation; they are not to be memorized and then imposed on the group process. Our main concern in this book is not to equip you with an arsenal of gimmicks but to encourage you to invent techniques that are extensions of yourself and your own sensitivities. We certainly are not urging you to memorize the techniques discussed in this book; rather, we hope that you use the book as a tool for enhancing your own abilities to generate techniques and to think through the reasons for and likely consequences of the techniques you invent.

Rather than going directly on to Chapter 2 now, you will find it useful, we believe, to turn instead to Chapter 7, the final chapter in the book. The outline of key ideas and concepts in that chapter provides a good review of the material we have covered in this first chapter. Reading Chapter 7 at this point will provide you with an overview of the points we will expand on in the remainder of the book and with a basis for understanding our philosophy and the way we lead groups.

QUESTIONS AND ACTIVITIES

At the end of each chapter we include a section of questions and activities. We hope you will use these sections to review the chapter and to clarify your own positions and integrate what you have read. Or you may prefer to spend your time thinking about issues we have not included. We list far more questions and activities than we think anyone will be interested in pursuing in depth. We encourage you to read all the questions and then select the ones that have the most interest and value for you, modifying them to match your own interests, client population, and situation. If you are using this book as a classroom text, many of the questions and activities listed can be adapted for small-group discussion, role playing, essay questions, and debates. The activities can be tried out in experiential groups.

As you review each chapter, you may have thoughts about how it could have been made clearer or more comprehensive. We hope that you will send us your reactions. You will find at the end of this book a form on which you can share your reactions with us. Mail it directly to us at Brooks/Cole, Monterey, California 93940.

1. How would you define a technique? How is a gimmick different from a technique?
2. As a group leader, to what extent do you use techniques, and when do you think it is appropriate or inappropriate to do so? How does your use of techniques fit with your overall view of what a group is for?
3. We stated some of our concerns about being too technique oriented. What are your concerns on this issue?
4. We take the position that there are more important factors in group work than techniques. If you agree, what do you think these factors are?
5. What do you think about approaching a group with a preset agenda versus letting the group take its own course? Give an example of a population for which a preset agenda might be appropriate.
6. What are your ideas about using preplanned group exercises and techniques as a means of stimulating interaction in a group?
7. Give some examples of how techniques might interfere with group process.
8. Think of some examples of being inflexible in using techniques.
9. How would you announce to a group that a technique you introduced is not working?
10. As a group leader, to what degree do you see yourself as structuring and directing the groups you lead, and how would your employment of techniques reflect this structure?
11. We spoke of the importance of the relationship between leader and client. What are some of the ways in which this relationship can be obscured through the use of techniques?
12. How do you view client defenses? Do you see it as appropriate to always break down these defenses?
13. What is your theory of group work, and what is the proper role of techniques in light of that theory?
14. When and how might you explain to a client your rationale for suggesting a technique? What would you not tell a member about a technique?
15. What is your understanding of resistance? Do you see resistance simply as something to be gotten around? Why or why not? Do you see resistance as unwillingness to work? How might you work with resistance?
16. What sorts of techniques would you not use with a psychotic population? an adolescent population? a group of children? a group of elderly persons? a group composed of sociopaths?
17. We stressed the importance of the personal characteristics of the

group leader. What are your thoughts on this matter? What do you see as the most important characteristics for group leaders?

18. Given your own characteristics and experience, why do you think you have a right to counsel others? Suppose a member of a group you were leading asked you this question. What might you say?

19. If you have no faith in the group modality, how might this attitude affect the outcome for a group you are leading?

20. Have you participated in a group as a member? What did this experience teach you about yourself? about group process? about leading groups?

21. What sorts of clues do you think would typically form the basis for a hunch of yours about introducing a technique with a particular person?

22. How important is it for you that a technique you introduce work out to be right or appropriate? What inhibits you from trying various techniques?

23. What topics would you like to have seen added to this chapter, and what would you have said about them?

We suggest that you begin each chapter by reading through and thinking about these questions. Then, after finishing each chapter, reread the questions and select the ones you'd like to consider further or discuss in class.

CHAPTER TWO

Ethical Considerations in Using Group Techniques

Before turning to specific techniques, we would like in this chapter to discuss some ethical concerns about the use of techniques in group work. Techniques are powerful instruments. Their abuse is not always due to a lack of concern for members; it can also come from a lack of awareness of the potential effects of techniques. This chapter concerns the responsible use of techniques in group work. We do not attempt to address the broad ethical issues of group work; we are concerned here mainly with specific issues posed by the use of techniques.

In this book, we encourage you as a group leader to show spontaneity and inventiveness in the use of techniques. We are excited about urging you to invent and yet feel a need to urge you also to strike a balance between this creativity and an irresponsible lack of caution.

We want to share some of our own excitement and creativity in working with groups, and yet we fear that we may contribute to an attitude about techniques that may lead to their being abused. We believe that the reputation of group counseling has suffered from irresponsible practitioners, mostly those who use techniques in a gimmicky, ill-conceived, or inappropriate way. But we do not want to foster the dangerous myth that there is a whole tidy body of techniques firmly embedded in clear-cut scientific doctrine, guaranteed to lead to highly predictable outcomes when used by omniscient specialists. Neither do we want people to become overly rigid and frightened in their group leadership. Basically, we believe that if you have a sound academic background, have had extensive supervised group experience, have had your own therapy, and have a fundamental respect for your clients, you are not likely to abuse techniques.

This chapter deals with ethical issues pertaining to group preparation and norms (providing information about the leader, about the structure and function of the group, about basic policies); ethical issues pertaining to the leader's motivations and theoretical stance (the misuse of techniques in a variety of forms as well as the leader's being able to provide a rationale for the techniques employed); ethical issues in using techniques as avoidance devices (such as avoiding dealing with members directly or avoiding material with which the leader feels uncomfortable); ethical issues relating to undue pressure (pressure from peers and leaders to participate, misuse of aggressive and confrontational techniques, forced touching, and inappropriate catharsis); ethical issues involved in protecting members when physical techniques are used; and ethical considerations in the use of the coleadership model.

Group preparation and norms

Providing information about the group. The techniques appropriate for a group depend on the goals and on the qualifications of the leader. Prospective members and referring agencies should be informed about these goals and qualifications. If the group is advertised to the general public, then the particular population or theme or counseling modality for which the group is designed should be made clear. Is it to be a self-awareness group for singles, a support group for persons recently widowed, a behavior modification group for adolescents with school-related difficulties? Is it going to have a limited number of sessions, or might the group continue as long as there is interest? All these goals need to be made clear in advance.

Prospective clients should also be informed about the professional qualifications of the leaders. We do not endorse the view that leaders must possess advanced academic degrees and be, for instance, licensed psychologists with a specialty in group work. We do believe that group leaders should have had academic training in a discipline related to human behavior, in-depth personal therapy, and extensive supervised group work. In addition, it is important that group leaders have a realistic perspective of the limitations of their own training gained from evaluations of their abilities by supervisors and professionals.

As far as is feasible, the kinds of techniques leaders are likely to employ should be explained to prospective members and these techniques should be congruent with the leaders' level of training and experience. Leaders should not suppose that the mere possession of relevant academic degrees and licenses guarantees that they are personally or experientially qualified for employing any technique, and they should not suppose that citing such degrees is sufficient for fully informing prospective clients about their qualifications. If emphasis is going to be on some specialized techniques, such as Rolfing or primal screaming, for which there are recognized trainers or workshops, it is appropriate for the leaders to indicate that they have worked with these trainers or attended these workshops. Leaders who cannot substantiate their training in the specialized techniques they plan to emphasize in their groups may be misleading prospective clients.

In setting group goals and identifying proposed techniques, leaders should be aware that the material they wish to explore should connect with issues they have looked at in their own lives. And while they may not have experienced every specific technique they intend to use, they should have personally experienced the general kinds of techniques they want to employ or should have learned about them under the supervision of or in collaboration with someone familiar with them.

Although group members should be informed in advance about the kinds of procedures and techniques that are likely to be employed in the group, it would be unrealistic to try to explain every technique in advance. But group members can be informed about the general style of the leader. Certainly, if the leader intends to employ exotic techniques such as nudity, highly cathartic techniques such as heavy-breathing, emotional-release procedures, or aggressive techniques designed to break down resistances, the client should be fully aware of these intentions. For example, in one group the leader informed the members in the middle of a session that they were going to take off their clothes and talk about body images. One member objected and was subjected to considerable peer pressure and to the leader's assurance that it would be good for him. While we are not necessarily opposed to nudity, we think it completely inappropriate to introduce it into a group when members have not been prepared for it. Here the issue amounts to having some sensitivity for what clients have a right to know when they are deciding whether to join a group.

Some of these considerations can be addressed in literature or advertising about the group. We believe that one of the best times to inform prospective group members about the goals of the group and the training of the leader is during screening and interviewing, which we discuss in the next chapter.

Using videotapes and audiotapes. Recording devices (tape recorders and videotapes) are commonly used for training purposes as well as for giving feedback to members. We think it essential that no recordings be made without the knowledge and consent of the members of the group. Members should know why the session is being recorded or videotaped, what will become of the material, and how it will be used. If the tapes will be used for research or will be listened to or seen and critiqued by a supervisor and students in a practicum, the members have a right to be informed of this use. At times an individual member might want to tape-record his or her work in a session, but the recorder should be turned off after that person's piece of work, and the other members should agree to the use of the device.

Leaders often find it useful to videotape a group session and allow members to view the tape sometime before the next session; this is an excellent feedback device. Such a tape can eventually be erased, and it can be agreed that it will be used only by the group members and the leaders. If recording devices are used in this way, it is a good policy to inform members that they can stop the machine any time they feel it is inhibiting their participation.

Perhaps it should be noted here that some members find it difficult to cope with feelings aroused by reviewing alone a recording made of their part in a session. Leaders may want to exercise caution about making such recordings available to members between sessions. In any case, the leader's policies about such matters should be known ahead of time by the prospective members.

Granting the freedom to leave.   Some leaders contend that members should always have the right to leave a group, and others feel strongly that once members have committed themselves to a group they have an obligation to stay with it. The leader's attitudes and policies about this topic should be spelled out at the onset of a group or, better, at a preliminary session. Our position is that clients have a responsibility to the leaders and members to explain why they want to leave. We have several reasons for this policy. It can be deleterious to members to leave without being able to discuss what they considered threatening or negative in the experience; and, in addition, it is unfortunate for members to leave a group because of a misunderstanding about some feedback they have received. On the other side, it can be damaging to other members if they suppose that someone left the group because of something they said or did. By having the person who is leaving present reasons to the group as a whole, we give the other members an opportunity to check out any concerns they may have about their responsibility for that person's decision. We tell our members that they have an obligation to attend all sessions and to inform us and the group should they decide to withdraw. If members even consider withdrawing, we encourage them to say so because such an acknowledgment inevitably provides extremely important material to work with. While we do not seek to subject members to a debate or to undue pressure to stay, we do stress the serious impact their leaving will have on the whole group, especially if they do so without explanation.

The leader's motivations and theoretical stance

Being aware of motivations.   We are concerned about leaders who use techniques to protect themselves or to meet their own needs for power or prestige or to control the members of their groups. Group leaders who are unaware of their motivations can misuse techniques in various ways: They may apply pressure on certain individuals to get them to perform in desired ways. They may use techniques mainly to impress participants with their therapeutic prowess. They may steer members away from explorations of feelings and issues they personally find threatening. They may use highly confrontive techniques and exercises to stir up aggression in their groups. In all such cases, the leader's needs become primary, while those of the members assume relative unimportance.

The potential exists for leaders to hide behind their position. They can camouflage their incompetence, fearfulness, or insecurity by seeking to create the impression that they are all-knowing and all-powerful. They can keep their real feelings hidden and project only what is consistent with the impression they wish to create; and they can choose techniques that perpetuate this illusion.

Even experienced leaders are sometimes slow to recognize such motivations in their use of various techniques. When these become patterns, one hopes they will show up in the leaders' own therapy or supervision sessions. Coleaders can also point out these patterns. If leaders do not have supervisors or coleaders, they should make a habit of reviewing group sessions and be alert to ways their own needs and motives may be getting in the way.

Dealing with the superhuman image.   Group members often attribute exaggerated power and wisdom to leaders, and there is a temptation for leaders who are motivated by a need for power to unethically reinforce this misconception. One way to avoid such reinforcement is to be willing to explain the purpose of a suggested technique. Although it is distracting to regularly explain the point of a technique in advance, it can, on occasion, be appropriate for a member to ask and for a leader to state what a technique is for. For instance, Jim says that he feels cut off and lonely in the group. When the leader requests that he go into the next room, Jim asks for a reason. Rather than insisting that he "just do it" the leader can supply a brief explanation: "I'd like you to have some sense of what it would be like to accentuate your feeling of being cut off so that we can explore that." At this point the leader may not want to explain certain other reasons for using the technique. For instance, the leader may have a hunch that Jim was typically sent out of the room as a child and that this exercise will bring back those feelings and allow connections between them and his current loneliness to emerge. The hunch would be sabotaged by explaining it at the beginning, but it can be explained afterward if need be. Explaining techniques in this way tends to discredit the impression that leaders are superhuman wizards.

Having a theoretical rationale.   Leaders can't always predict the exact outcomes of techniques, but they can have some expected outcomes in mind, and they can have some idea of how a technique is connected with the material of the moment. If a supervisor or a colleague or a group member asks a leader "Why did you use that technique? What did you hope to gain from it?" the leader should be able to justify using it. A leader who cannot do so is probably grasping at straws and filling time rather than providing constructive leadership. We are not urging leaders to be so preoccupied with thinking about the rationale for a technique that they become timid and unspontaneous, but being aware of the purpose of a technique can become second nature and does not have to be incompatible with the ability to spontaneously follow a hunch.

The rationale for using a technique should be rooted in the whole picture of what the client has revealed. No counselor is going to remember every clue, of course. But every effort should be made to remember key themes from different episodes in the client's work. For example, one week Bill talked about his fear of becoming involved in an intimate relationship. In another session Bill was uninvolved in the group: he sprawled in his chair and seemed about to fall asleep. During another meeting, he said he felt he was treated coldly by others in the group. The leader remembered these episodes; she attempted to bring them together by inviting Bill to sprawl out and look sleepily around the room, saying to each member a whole sentence that started "A way I keep myself removed from you is. . . ." In this example the leader had a rationale—she sought to connect already existing material with the direction the technique was likely to take.

Using techniques as avoidance devices

Avoiding a member's confrontation.   In a recent workshop, we witnessed a client attempting to express a legitimate concern to the therapist. The client was asked to pretend that the therapist was in an empty chair and to direct his concerns to the chair rather than to the therapist directly. Such avoidance of dealing directly with a client raises an ethical issue about the therapist's willingness to have honest inter-action with clients. It implies that clients have no legitimate issues with the group leader, that what they have to say is only neurotic transfer-ence. In another frequent interchange a client expresses anger toward the leader, and the leader responds "I'm glad you can get your feelings out."Such a response is condescending and suggests that the leader is preserving self-esteem at the expense of encountering clients. People cannot enhance their humanness if they are led to believe that their group leaders are better than human.

Avoiding the leader's fears.   Some leaders introduce tech-niques to cover up their own fears or unwillingness to explore the themes that are present in the group. Such diversion frequently occurs with themes relating to lack of closeness and hostility.

If closeness in a group is to be genuine, it takes time to develop; during some periods in a group's history closeness is often conspicuously absent. If leaders feel uncomfortable with this lack of closeness, they may try to force a false sense of closeness through the use of various techniques. For example, in one group with an apparent lack of close-ness, the leader suggested that the members all huddle together. If any technique is to be introduced here, we believe it preferable to suggest that the members of the group spread apart, to far corners of the room, and then be asked to talk about how they feel. In other words, leaders should attempt to make explicit and even exaggerate what is already going on rather than trying to overcome their own uncomfortableness by imposing an artificial solution.

In another group the leader requested two hostile members to shake hands and speak positively to each other. He asked them to pretend that the conflict did not exist rather than to explore what it was about. As a result of the leader's uncomfortableness, they did not get to the real issues between them. When conflict exists within a group, we think it should be acknowledged directly and dealt with openly. If conflict is not brought into the open, it lies dormant and festers, and eventually pro-ductive work in the group halts.

A related abuse of techniques to avoid the leader's uncomfortableness often occurs during awkward moments in groups. For example, the group may be lethargic, silences may be long, members may initiate little, and resistance may be manifested in several forms. At times like these we urge leaders to deal directly with this phenomenon. In a desperate attempt to get things moving some leaders suggest an interaction technique or call on members directly and ask them questions. We think that these techniques cover up potentially rich material; resorting to techniques to avoid this material is typically a manifestation of leader anxiety.

A broad way of stating the ethical concern here is this: One of the most important things a group can and should teach is that we can learn to face and express what we think and feel. If group leaders introduce techniques that detract from or cover up the dynamics of the group, then they are modeling the idea that our feelings are something to be avoided.

In summary, one should be cautious about using techniques at all if they are artificial substitutes for genuine exploration. In addition, when a technique is introduced, it should generally serve to highlight the emotional, cognitive, behavioral material present in the group and not to detract from it because of the leader's uncomfortableness.

Undue pressure

Freedom not to participate.   Some group leaders make frequent use of interaction exercises, communication exercises, and nonverbal exercises to promote group interaction. For example, a leader may ask members to pair up and engage in a touching exercise or to otherwise express what they are feeling to their partners in a nonverbal way. If leaders are not careful, they can easily create the impression that all members are expected to participate in all such exercises. Such leaders court the dangers of intruding on members' sensitivities and of not respecting their right to pass on some of the exercises that they might not want to participate in or might not be ready to handle. Leaders cannot simply state at the beginning of a group that members have a right not to participate if they choose not to do so, for some members may feel pressured to do what everyone else is doing. Leaders must make it genuinely acceptable for members to pass by mentioning this option periodically whenever it is appropriate.

To avoid this problem we usually invite members to work on personally meaningful material. If members bring up issues they want to work on, the chances are increased that they can handle whatever might surface.

Further, we typically impress on members that they can decide at what point they wish to stop. Members sometimes open up a painful or threatening area and then say that they do not want to go ahead. Generally, we explore their desire for stopping, and in this way we can focus on the factors members find threatening. They may not trust the leader to deal with what will come out. They may not trust the group enough to pursue an issue. They may be worried about looking foolish. They may fear losing control and not being able to regain composure. Even if members decide to stop, we tell them that if at a later time they want to return to the issue we hope that they will announce this desire. The responsibility is then clearly on the members to decide what they will bring out in the group and the level or depth to which they choose to explore the issues they do bring out. Placing responsibility with the members is a built-in safety factor, and it is a sign of our respect for them.

There is another side to this issue. We assume that people who come to a group want some pressure. So the tricky task is to achieve a balance between appropriate pressure and unethical coercion. A leader who is unwilling even to say "Are you really sure you are unwilling to do this?" or "How would it be if you just tried this for a minute, and then we could stop if you like?" may be failing to take some responsibility for maintaining a productive environment. The leader needs to be alert to whether the client is leaving an opening for pursuing the technique, but the leader also has an ethical obligation to respect the client's refusal. Our practice is to respect this refusal and yet to attempt to explore the client's reasons for declining.

In these cases, much depends on the make-up and purpose of a given group and even more depends on the relationship we have with a particular client. A developed relationship puts us in a position to know where some prodding might be in order. The ethical issue centers on having a basic respect for working with material that is already present and, even more important, a basic respect for the client's decisions about what to explore and how far to go with it.

Pressure from other members.   Group leaders have an ethical obligation to respond to undue peer pressure on a group member, especially when they have assured the group that no one will be coerced into making disclosures or participating in activities. The leader can comment on the peer pressure or can offer an interpretation of the seeming need to coerce and thus can turn the spotlight on the people exerting the pressure. The leader can ask them to talk about why they need to pressure another: "You seem intent on getting Jane to talk more. Would you tell her what you know about yourself that makes this so important to you?" "Would you tell the group how you are going to feel if you fail to get Jane to do as you wish?" "Would it be relevant for you to talk about relationships you have had outside this group in which you wish someone would do what you are trying to get Jane to do?" The point of such interventions is to acknowledge the feelings of those who are exerting the pressure and to see what productive work might be done with those feelings, while reminding the group of the need to respect the wishes of an unwilling member.

Misuse of confrontational techniques.   At times group leaders can abuse their power by directing techniques toward a particular group member. Some leaders derive a sense of power from putting members on the spot and bombarding them with questions or from deliberately putting them in a defensive position or from applying pressure on them to open up. One group leader we observed opened a session by calling on a particular member, and he stayed with this person for the entire session. He believed this was an effective technique to use with resistant members; he assumed such pressure would crack their stubborn defenses. In other groups the leader asks question after question and relies on this technique to give the group the appearance of movement. Although we think confrontational techniques can be used to work through members' resistances or defenses, we don't think it appropriate to endlessly interrogate members. When leaders resort to a barrage of questions, the members are likely to close themselves off. Other members tend to pick up the questioning behavior, the atmosphere of trust is lost, and members are deprived of the opportunity to explore issues in depth. Instead, they think only about how to make appropriate answers to the questions thrown at them. Confrontation needs to be handled with care and concern for the member being confronted; it is not to be used by leaders as a club to beat members into submission.

Forced touching.   There are several facets to the ethical issue of using touching as a technique. In some cases leaders use touching techniques to fulfill their own needs or fantasies and are not sensitive to the needs of group participants. Leaders may have a lack of touching and physical contact in their own lives, and they compensate for this lack through their work with groups.

Another ethical aspect of touching techniques has to do with their potential artificiality; they can often be used as a short cut to intimacy.

Some clients are not comfortable with being touched or regard a certain level of intimacy to be a condition for touching. Although increasing comfortableness with physical contact is therapeutically important (and the encounter-group movement recognized this fact in stressing touching), this need should be balanced by respect for the readiness and the values of the participants. We do not discourage spontaneous touching in our groups, but we rarely introduce a technique that explicitly directs clients into a physical intimacy they do not want. As a group develops intimacy and risk taking, touching tends to increase, but then the touching has been earned rather than imposed. If two members are struggling to get to know one another and to break through their usual boundaries, a touching technique is only likely to bypass the hard work that meaningful intimacy requires.

A final ethical facet of touching arises when a leader is asked to touch someone from whom the leader feels distant; such a request may arise, for example, when the leader is role-playing a mother or father. Group leaders have an obligation to be genuine in such cases, partly because of the harm that dishonesty has already done to many of their clients. Here the ethical issue is that of being honest with clients and of modeling honesty. Clients are likely to sense when leaders ignore their own reservations, and they are deprived of the opportunity for obtaining an explanation for the lack of closeness in their lives when they do not get straight feedback from the leader.

Inappropriate catharsis.   Some leaders are too ready to evaluate the success of their groups by the degree of emotional intensity they evoke and are too eager to push people into a cathartic experience for its own sake. Highly emotional sessions are exciting for their drama, and the expression of emotion is certainly an important component of the group process; the danger is in losing sight of what one hopes to have emerge from catharsis. Moreover, group leaders and members can acquire the expectation that every member should display intense emotion and is somehow a failure if he or she does not do so. We recall a group member who approached a leader during a break and stated tearfully that she must not be getting anything from the group because she hadn't yet had a catharsis.

Among the ethical issues that catharsis involves are questions such as these: Whose needs are being met with the catharsis—those of the leader, the group, or the individual member? Is the leader clear about what the catharsis is supposed to mean or is supposed to lead to? Is the leader capable of handling the intensity of the catharsis or what it might lead to? Is there enough time in the group session to work with the emotions that arise and to arrive at a resolution? Will the group leader have subsequent sessions with the client to deal with the repercussions of the catharsis? Is the leader sensitive to the subtle line between invoking catharsis for its therapeutic potential and invoking catharsis for the sake of drama?

Leaders should be especially aware of times they use catharsis to fulfill their own and not their clients' needs. Leaders may like to see people express anger because they would like to be able to do so themselves, for example, and so they unethically push members to get into contact with angry feelings by developing techniques to bring out such feelings and to focus the group on anger. Leaders can also develop techniques that push members to express only positive and warm feelings toward one another; that push members to regress into childhood and relive their loneliness; that stir up conflict within a group; or that keep conflict from being recognized and expressed in the group. The point is not that these are not legitimate feelings, for surely most members are at times angry, lonely, in conflict, or feeling rejected. The issue is the degree to which the leader's needs become central in the selection of techniques designed to bring out certain feelings in members.

Use of physical techniques

As with touching, the encounter-group movement fostered many techniques to help people express their aggressive feelings—hitting pillows, arm wrestling, pushing and shoving, breaking in or out of a circle; these techniques are often unpredictable in outcome. The symbolic release of aggression can obviously be valuable, but relevant precautions should be taken. Leaders who introduce such techniques should protect the client and the other members from harm and should be prepared to deal with unforeseen directions the exercise may take. The concern here is not simply for the physical safety of the clients. If a client has restrained emotion for a long time out of fear of the consequences of expressing it, that fear receives tragic reinforcement if the emotion does indeed get out of control when it is expressed and proves damaging to others. In general, we avoid physical techniques involving the whole group for reasons of safety; we prefer to introduce physical techniques only when pursuing work with an individual client with whom we are familiar.

Leaders who introduce such techniques should have enough experience and training to deal with the consequences. While we encourage leaders to try techniques, we also see a danger in their foolishly or unthinkingly using techniques they have not experienced themselves or in their using techniques that easily generate material that they have no idea how to handle. Merely reading about techniques and then trying them out is not sufficient. Beginning leaders should use them only when direct supervision is available or when they are coleading with an experienced counselor.

In addition, leaders should never goad or push members into physical exercises. Here, inviting members to participate in an exercise and giving them the clear option of refraining are essential. If leaders explain to members the exercise they have in mind, ask them whether they want to try it, and take safety precautions, chances for negative outcomes are minimized.

Let's look at some specific physical techniques in order to understand the risks involved in their use. Is the potential value of a technique worth the risk? This question is a good one to ask about all physical techniques, for, while they may be useful in evoking feelings or generating material, these benefits need to be balanced by the risks.

Falling backward.   One technique sometimes used to generate trust is to ask a member to fall backward and be caught by another member in the group. In general, we are reluctant to use this technique, for we'd rather deal directly with a member's lack of trust. If this technique is used, however, the person doing the catching must be physically able to do so because of the clear risk of back injury.

Holding onto a person.   At times a member may say something like "I just wish I could get my father off my back." One technique that can be used to accentuate her feelings of being burdened and held down by her father's expectations is for the leader to go behind her and grab onto her. The leader, speaking for her father, can say, "I'll never let go of you. I like you weak and helpless, and I'll always cling to you and keep you down." Clearly this exercise is designed to provoke her and to challenge her to throw her father off her back. If the leader is not careful and strong enough to deal with her potential physical aggression, the leader is likely to end up with bruises, rug burns, or even a broken bone or broken teeth.

Holding a person down or in.   In a related technique several group members hold one member down on the floor or form a tight circle and challenge the member to break out in any way possible. For the member lying on the floor, there are some clear dangers. Participants may have difficulty obtaining sufficient oxygen, they may hyperventilate, or they may overexert themselves to the point of heart failure. Clearly, even if members are willing to take part in such an exercise, leaders should know their medical histories and their current state of health. Other members can also be injured in their attempt to form a tight and confining circle and to keep the fighting member caged in.

In addition to the physical risks, such holding of a member can bring forth intense feelings—feelings the member may not be ready to deal with or feelings that may be beyond the ability of the group leader to work with effectively. Further, this technique may open up within the group intense feelings that the members may not be able to handle, especially if the leader does not know how to work with the feelings that have been uncorked. The key is for the leader to ascertain whether the group is ready to handle potentially explosive material and for the leader to be able to help all members effectively work through any feelings that are expressed.

Pushing, shoving, wrestling.   If a group leader wants to provoke a member into expressing anger, both verbally and nonverbally, the leader may use the technique of pushing. Here, the physical setting must be taken into account. One of us observed a beginning leader shoving and pushing a young man in the group he was leading. As he pushed, he chided the member about being weak and told him that he'd never be anything but a whimpering kid. He was using this technique in a rather small room with a large mirror made of thin glass. Either the member or the leader could easily have lost his balance and been pushed through the mirror. Either the leader was unaware of the potential hazards for physical injury, or his need for creating a dramatic event was greater than his appreciation of the potential danger.

If shoving or wrestling techniques are used, the rest of the members must protect those involved by being aware of sharp corners, protruding objects, and other hazards in the setting. Leaders should refrain from using such techniques unless they are both trained and physically able to handle the possible outcomes. Even if none of the members are injured, such exercises can have the negative effect of closing down members who may fear that they too could lose control or who may be frightened by the emotions unleashed; these fears should be explored fully in the group.

Highly cathartic body techniques.   Many leaders are presently interested in a variety of techniques sometimes referred to as neo-Reichian or emotional-release or bioenergetic techniques. These methods induce strong regressive and primal emotions, typically by coupling deep or rapid breathing with various postures or movements and by putting sounds with the breathing (moaning, shouting). These techniques are truly powerful, and the intense emotions they generate can be terrifying for the client or for other group members or even for the therapist working with such methods for the first time. Additionally, they do have some inherent physical dangers such as hyperventilation.

The central ethical issue is the competence of the leader. The leader who is not ready to deal with strong expressions of emotion ought not to be employing techniques likely to elicit them. A further concern is that the leader be sufficiently familiar with the client to have some basis for judging whether a technique that induces such catharsis is appropriate. These techniques should also be introduced when there is ample time, including follow-up time, for working through the material generated. We prefer not to employ these techniques for a whole group, but only as a means of working further with feelings that a client is already displaying and ready to intensify. We also do not introduce such techniques simply as a means of getting the group to move.

Coleadership

We favor coleadership for a number of reasons. Having more than one leader increases the ways in which a group can function. Especially with a female/male team, members can benefit from having two role models. Members can also benefit from being exposed to two or more leadership styles, and they can benefit from the differing perceptions of different coleaders. A technique that we use when we are coleading a group or a workshop is to talk out loud with each other about what we are observing and experiencing in the group. This gives the members an opportunity to gauge our reactions. For example, if the group seems to be going nowhere, the coleaders might talk to each other briefly about this situation and share their feelings about it openly. Coleaders can also talk about what they think the group needs or a direction in which they think the group should move.

From the vantage point of the coleaders, each can build on the other's style, and they can complement and extend each other's work with individuals. Coleaders can provide each other with valuable feedback after each session, and they can share impressions of what occurred in the group. They can bring two perspectives to the understanding of certain individuals or particular relationships in the group, and they can work together on plans for further directions of the group sessions.

An ethical issue arises when coleaders form a toxic relationship that inhibits the group's progress. For instance, group leaders who have sharp differences may ask the group to pick sides. Or coleaders who are competitive may push members into using techniques designed simply to prove the prowess of one or the other of the leaders.

To avoid these problems coleaders need to establish a relationship based on trust, cooperation, and respect—one in which each leader can function as an individual, yet one that is characterized by harmony and teamwork with both coleaders working for the good of the members. In such a relationship, the primary aim is not the fulfillment of the leaders' needs but the provision of diversity for the members.

Concluding comments

In this chapter, we have covered important ethical questions connected with the use of techniques in groups. The most important point we have made is that techniques can be harmful if used inappropriately or insensitively. They can injure group participants physically or emotionally. Ethical concerns arise when techniques are used simply as gimmicks and are not designed to serve the needs of the participants. The negative popular image of groups has come from the abuse of techniques, from using them to replace what a group fundamentally is—an arena for genuine and caring human interaction.

QUESTIONS AND ACTIVITIES

1. What kind of information do you think you should give potential clients before they enter a group, and what, if anything, do you think you ought not to inform them about?
2. What was your reaction to the following statement? "Basically, we believe that if you have a sound academic background, have had extensive supervised group experience, have had your own therapy, and have a fundamental respect for your clients, you are not likely to abuse techniques."
3. Imagine a setting in which a group member declines to participate in a technique or exercise you suggest. Describe how you would want to respond. How might this refusal have different implications depending on the stage of the group's development?
4. Describe a specific context and client, and explain how you would respond to the client's asking "What is this technique supposed to accomplish?"
5. We hold that leaders should have a theoretical rationale to support their choice of a technique. Do you agree? Think of some specific techniques you have used in leading a group. What was your rationale for using them?
6. Think of a situation in which a conflict is not being openly expressed within the group. What do you think you would do?

How might using a technique in this situation mask a leader's fears about his or her own competence?

7. How do you teach your group members to confront in a constructive manner? What are the differences between confrontation and attack?

8. Do you think that psychological risks are necessarily a part of group participation? Explain. What are some major risks related to group work? What kinds of safeguards might you take to minimize such risks?

9. A client is following a technique you have introduced and then says that she wants to stop. Would you be inclined to explore with her the reasons for wanting to stop? Why or why not?

10. Under what circumstances and with what conditions do you believe it appropriate for a member to leave a group? Explain your position.

11. How would you explain to a group the importance of confidentiality? Are there any techniques you might use in connection with this explanation?

12. What are some ways techniques might be misused that we have not talked about?

13. Describe what you regard as unethical motivations for using a technique.

14. As a leader, what advantages do you see to being self-disclosing? To creating an aura of mystery about yourself? Mention several ways that a group leader might hide behind the role of leader.

15. A member says to you: "I don't know you. I want to have you share more of yourself personally so that I can trust you." How might you respond?

16. How do you feel about confronting a member? When do you think you should do so, in what manner, and why? What are your guidelines for constructive confrontation?

17. What considerations do you think are important in deciding whether a leader should touch a client?

18. If you think it is wrong for you to have a sexual relationship with a group member, give your reasons.

19. You observe that several members of your group are pressuring an individual to say or do something. How do you think you might respond in this situation?

20. Explain your position on preplanned exercises involving touching. How would you deal with a situation in which one or more members objected to being touched? If you did introduce exercises involving touching, what would be your reasons for doing so?

21. Suppose a member of your group declares that it would be helpful

for him to wrestle with another member. What concerns might you have, and how might you handle the request?

22. Assume that a member is engaged in a physical exercise involving aggression and declares that she feels panic stricken and unable to breathe. What might be going on, and what would you do?

23. Explain your position regarding techniques in which one member is physically aggressive with another as opposed to techniques using an inanimate object as the target for aggressive feelings.

24. A member who has been following your suggested technique says she feels a tingling in her arms, lightheaded, and numb. What might she be describing? How would you deal with this situation?

25. Do you think you should have experienced a technique yourself before you introduce it in a group? Explain.

26. We have urged you to be cautious on a number of grounds, and we have also encouraged you to be creative in your use of techniques. What would you describe as your own guidelines for reconciling these two seemingly contradictory suggestions? When should creativity yield to caution?

27. You find yourself introducing many techniques involving physical touching and physical closeness. How would you try to determine whether you were mainly meeting your own needs or responding to material the group wanted to explore?

28. In what ways can you fulfill your own desires and needs while you are a leader of a group? What problems do you see if you rely on your work as a group leader to meet your needs?

29. What do you see as the potential advantages and the potential hazards of coleading?

30. Assume that you are having negative reactions toward your coleader during a group session. What might you do?

31. What kinds of matters do you see as most important to discuss with your coleader before and after a group meeting?

32. Suppose you find yourself being protective of your coleader. What do you think this situation might indicate about you, and what effect might it have on your group?

33. What are your thoughts on the training and supervision necessary for group leadership and the use of group techniques? What are some of the most important ingredients in a training program for group leaders?

34. Assume that you are a member of a committee that is drafting guidelines for training standards. Some members claim that an essential part of the training of group leaders is membership in a personal-growth or counseling group. What is your position? If you

were to be a part of such a therapy group, what personal issues do you think you would most want to explore?

35. Explain what you believe to be the most important ethical considerations regarding group techniques. Are any of them ones that we have failed to discuss in this chapter?

CHAPTER THREE

Techniques for Preparing Groups

This chapter discusses techniques designed to prepare group members for effective work as well as practical ways to get groups started. In our group work, we believe in clarifying both leader and member expectations from the outset. Members have a right to know the goals and procedures of a group, and they should be informed about their rights and responsibilities as members and the expectations leaders have for them. We also believe that members get the most from a group experience if leaders do some teaching about group process at the beginning.

In this chapter we share some of the ways we have found for getting groups established. We also describe issues involved in and techniques for recruiting, screening, selecting, and preparing members. In preparing members a preliminary group session can be effective for orientation purposes. We find that if members are inadequately prepared groups often get stuck in the initial stage because they are unable to work through conflicts that result from a lack of basic information. In our view, using the techniques described in this chapter is one of the best ways of ensuring that a group will move forward and be productive.

Getting groups established

A difficult and demanding part of leading a group is the work needed to make a group come into existence. In an organized setting—a school, a mental health agency, a mental hospital, a clinic—approval is usually needed to organize a group. In such situations and also when starting groups outside of organized settings, you will find it helpful to write a proposal that clarifies your goals. If the goals are vague, chances are the director of the setting or the potential members will not receive the idea for a group enthusiastically. With a well thought-out proposal you can sell potential participants or directors on the value of a group program. In addition, a carefully written proposal can prevent the confusion and misunderstanding that often have deleterious effects on how groups function.

In writing a proposal you should cover the following points:

- What kind of group will this be? What kind of structure will the group have?
- What will the leader's function in the group be?
- Why is a group the best approach to take in this situation? What are the unique properties of a group that make it valuable here?
- For whom is the group designed?
- What will the main goals of the group be?
- Who will lead and colead the group? What are their qualifications? Their backgrounds? Their experience?
- Where will the group be held? How long will it last?
- What topics will be explored?
- How will the potential dangers or risks of group participation be dealt with?
- What kind of evaluation procedures will be used to determine the degree to which the goals of the group are met?
- What kind of follow-up procedures will be used to help members integrate what they learn and evaluate this learning?

It is useful to present proposals to colleagues or even to a neighbor. Such a trial run provides the opportunity to revise the plan so that it has an increased chance of being accepted.

The sample proposal in the box illustrates how to put a sharp focus on the goals, structure, and format of a group for the benefit of program directors and of potential participants in the group.

PROPOSAL FOR AN ADOLESCENT GROUP

I. Type of Group
This will be a personal-growth and self-exploration group for young people between the ages of 15 and 18. The group will *not* be a therapy group aimed

at treating the severly disturbed; instead it will focus on the problems and concerns of the typical adolescent. The group will meet for a limited time as follows:

1. Three meetings once a week during the evening from 6:30 to 9:30.
2. An all-day meeting on Saturday from 9:00 A.M. to 5:00 P.M.
3. A follow-up meeting during an evening from 6:30 to 9:30.

During the initial session the leader will give specific suggestions to assist the participants in getting the *most* from their group experience. During this initial meeting the focus will be on getting acquainted, developing a climate of trust, discussing possible topics for group exploration, and learning how to function productively as a group member.

This is a pilot project. At the follow-up meeting the members and the leader will determine whether they want another series of group sessions.

Specific dates and fees.

II. Goals and Objectives

The group will be a place for self-exploration; participants will be invited to examine their values, behaviors, and relationships with others, to take a serious and honest look at the quality of their lives. The members will decide *what, how much,* and *when* to share of themselves, and they will *decide for themselves* the nature and extent of changes they want to make. However, participants are expected to be active members in the group.

Specific goals for group participants are as follows:

1. To develop sufficient trust of the group to allow for an honest sharing of feelings and attitudes, and to learn how to carry this trust into everyday life
2. To grow in self-acceptance and self-respect
3. To become tolerant of others, to respect others' differences
4. To learn how to make decisions and accept the consequences
5. To become less isolated by discovering that others in the group have similar problems
6. To clarify values and to begin to develop a philosophy of life
7. To increase the capacity to care for others
8. To become sensitive to the needs of others
9. To learn specific ways of applying in everyday life what is learned in the group

III. Rationale

Adolescents can grow as the result of openly and honestly exploring their concerns and learning how to become independent. They need to learn how to cope with their increasing freedom and the responsibilities that accompany it. Adolescents have both an interest in struggling to develop a personal identity and a need to do so in a setting that encourages honest self-exploration.

IV.   Group Leader
Name(s) of the group leader(s), degrees, professional and personal backgrounds and experiences, qualifications for leading groups, and other pertinent information.

V.   Basic Ground Rules
1. Members must come to all the sessions and participate by sharing of themselves and giving feedback to others in the group.
2. Members must maintain the confidences of other group members.
3. Members may decide on their own specific goals and on the issues they want and are willing to explore.
4. Members may not smoke during group meetings.
5. Members must have the written concent of their parents to participate in the group.

VI. Topics for Group Exploration
The themes to be explored will be related to the adolescent's struggle toward autonomy and search for identity. Certain topics will be given emphasis, but group members will have the opportunity to discuss the aspects of those topics that are most meaningful to them. Below is a sample of some possible topics for group exploration. Other topics of concern to group participants can be developed.

1. Finding meaning in life and deciding on values
2. Being alone
3. Being with others
4. Love, sex, intimacy
5. Sex roles
6. Autonomy
7. School and work life

Recruiting members

Personal contact with the leader is the best way to recruit potential candidates for a group because members are committing themselves to working with a specific person. In addition, through personal contact the leader can enthusiastically demonstrate that the group has potential value for a person.

Rather than simply relying on flyers, leaders might contact people who can direct clients to them: colleagues, directors of clinics, teachers and professors, physicians, ministers, school counselors, psychologists, and social workers.

In the recruitment process, potential clients have a right to know the goals of the group, the basic procedures to be used, what will be expected of them as participants, what they can expect of the leader, and any major risks as well as potential values of participating in the group.

Screening and selecting members

The next step is to determine who might profit from the group and who (if anyone) should be excluded. One technique for making these decisions is to meet privately with every person who wishes to join the group. In such a meeting the leader can get a sense of the appropriateness of including a particular person in a group and can give the prospective member a chance to determine whether he or she wants to be involved. Leaders might keep in mind that all groups are not appropriate for all people. Indeed, for some, group participation can be damaging or at least counterproductive to their growth. The question of the appropriateness of including a member is directly related to the purpose and goals of the group. With these goals in mind a leader might use questions such as the following to guide the course of a half-hour individual session with the applicant:

- Why does this person want to join the group?
- How ready does the person seem to be to look at himself or herself and consider making changes?
- What does the candidate hope to get from the group? Will this group help the person achieve these goals?
- What does the prospective participant want to know about the leader or the group?
- Does the person understand the purposes and nature of the group?
- Are there any indications that a group would be counterproductive for this person?

This individual contact between the member and the leader can be extremely useful as a way to begin to establish trust, for this session can allay fears and can provide the foundation for future work. Of course, orientation interviews are time consuming and may not always be feasible, but they are worth the time that they take. Even a brief contact significantly reduces risk and contributes to the overall quality of the group. The individual members have some idea of what to expect; they are likely to come prepared to work; and they are likely to feel subsequently that the leader recognizes them as individuals within the group.

A valuable procedure is to meet again for a private session after the termination of the group to assess what each person is taking away from the group, to talk about particular plans for continued work, and to discuss plans for implementing what was learned in the group. The screening interview helps people establish their specific goals; the final interview helps them evaluate the degree to which these goals were met.

Conducting a preliminary session

In addition to a meeting with each applicant on an individual basis prior to selection for membership in the group, we recommend a preliminary meeting with the potential members. The primary purpose of this meeting is for the leader to outline the purposes of the group in detail as well as to clarify what the participants will be doing in the group. It gives participants an opportunity to meet each other and to get additional data for making their decision about committing themselves to the group.

Such a meeting has the following specific purposes: getting acquainted; clarifying personal goals and group goals; learning about the procedures to be used in the group; learning about how the group will function and how to get the most from the experience; discussing the possible dangers or risks involved in participating in the group as well as ways of minimizing these risks; discussing the essential requirement of confidentiality and any other ground rules necessary for the effective functioning of the group; exploring with members their fears, expectations, hopes, and ambivalent feelings and answering their questions.

At the end of the first session, members can be asked to think about whether they want to join the group; and a leader who has reservations about admitting a member can arrange for another interview to explore these reservations.

Let's look at specific matters that need to be openly explored at the preliminary session (and then again perhaps during the initial meeting). One is the matter of confidentiality. Members will not feel free to explore issues in a meaningful way if they don't have the assurance that what they say will be held in confidence by both the leaders and the other members. Members need to be reminded emphatically about how easily they may unintentionally breach the confidences of other members by talking about specifics brought up in the group. For the leaders, it's important to state directly and openly any limitations of confidentiality.

Leaders should inform members of the circumstances under which they will have to divulge material that is brought up in the group. Such a statement is especially important in a mandatory group in a detention facility. For example, if a group leader must report on the clients' progress, the leader should clearly point out this requirement and make it a topic for discussion.

Other basic matters that might be mentioned at the preliminary session include policies on matters such as smoking or eating in the group; coming to the group on time; missing group sessions; socializing outside the group and other subgrouping matters; and having sessions recorded.

The best technique here is for the leader to simply state some essential procedures and policies and discuss them in the group. In addition, the leader can distribute two copies of a list of the important group procedures and policies to each member. Members can sign both copies, keeping one and giving the other to the group leader. Leaders who use this technique as a way of clarifying and focusing on procedures and policies they deem essential should go over the policies with the members and express the reasons for establishing them. The box contains a typical list of ground rules for a group.

GROUND RULES

1. Members are not to use drugs during a session and are not to come to a session under the influence of drugs.
2. Members are expected to be present at all the group meetings because their absence affects the entire group.
3. Members must avoid sexual involvements with others in the group during its duration.
4. Members are not to use physical violence in group sessions nor are they to be verbally abusive to others in the group.
5. Members will be given a summary of their rights and responsibilities so that they know what is expected of them before they join the group.
6. Members must keep confidential what other members do and say within the group.

On this last point, leaders might talk at some length of the ways in which confidentiality can be broken by members, both deliberately and unthinkingly.

Because of time restraints, a preliminary session may not be feasible in all cases, even though it is highly recommended. As a substitute, group leaders can integrate many of the ideas we cover here into the first session; the initial group meeting can then be an orientation session during which members can decide whether the group is appropriate for them.

Preparing parents of minors

In planning a group composed of children or adolescents, you should contact the parents of the potential members and secure their written permission before allowing the members to enroll in the group. This procedure can be done in a way that enhances the group process. For example, you can write a letter that describes the purposes of the group, the techniques that may be used, and the topics that may be explored. Parents can be asked to sign and return the letter.

An additional technique is to invite parents to a meeting with you so that you can present the need for such a group and the potential advantages and so that you can discuss questions or concerns that parents may have. Sending letters and holding a meeting with the parents can prevent many problems from erupting later. Parents who are not informed or whose cooperation is not enlisted can have their child removed from the group and can encourage the school or other institution not to allow such groups in the future. In addition, an honest presentation by you can put to rest some of the false notions parents may have about the group. For example, some parents may think that they will be the focus of group discussion, that family matters will be publicly aired, or that their children will be brainwashed.

Setting goals

Members and leaders should set goals for themselves both at the start of a group and at the start of each session if maximum learning is to occur. Members can begin to set these goals at the screening interview and also at the preliminary session. We describe in this section some techniques the leader may want to use in this goal-setting process. We hope that readers will not consider the activities we describe as school assignments but as focusing methods. These are merely suggestions to choose from; a leader would not want to use all these techniques in one group.

The kind of preparation we discuss here can be used in any group but is particularly useful in giving direction to groups, such as those for children, that may need a significant degree of structure in order to function effectively. A balance needs to be maintained between too much and not enough structure; too much structure may squelch the

creativity and self-direction of group members, yet not enough preparation may lead a group to flounder needlessly because of a lack of
focus. Another factor to consider in deciding on the degree of structure
is the leader's experience, training, and personal characteristics. Some
leaders work better with more structure, some with less.

A leader will have goals in mind for a group. These can be general
goals that have to do with establishing an environment within which
members can attain their personal goals. And they can be process goals
such as learning appropriate self-disclosure, being willing to share feelings, being willing to talk in a personal way, staying in the here-and-
now, expressing reactions to what is going on in the group, learning
how to confront with care and respect, and learning how to give others
feedback. If members know these goals from the start, they have a clear
idea of what is expected of them and also of how they might get the
most from the group for themselves.

In addition, members should clarify what they want from a group.
Often their thinking on this matter is fuzzy and global. They hope to
get in touch with their feelings; they would like to communicate better;
or they want to work on understanding themselves. These vague goals
are hard to work on in a group. Helping members translate these broad
goals into specific ones is the first step in preparation. Thus, if a member
says "I want to learn how to express my feelings," the leader might ask:
"What particular feeling do you have the most trouble expressing? In
what situations do you find it most difficult to express this feeling?
What's it like for you to be this way? How would you like to be different?"

Preparing contracts.   Asking members to tell each other of their
specific goals is one way to get them to think about their reasons for
being in the group. Having them write down these goals is valuable.
One technique is to ask people to write down what they'd most hope
to be able to say when the group ends. They then put their statements
in envelopes and read them at the last session to determine how close
they came to meeting those goals. A variation is to ask people to write
down at an early session what they'd like to have done or who they'd
like to have become or how they'd like to have changed in six months
or a year. They give these statements to the leader in self-addressed,
stamped envelopes, and the leader mails them unopened at the end of
the time period. Not only do such exercises challenge members to look
at what they want for themselves but they are also a device for accountability.

The full contract is an extension of such exercises. In full contracts
members write out the specific behaviors or attitudes they want to

change and what they are willing to do in and outside the group to make these changes. Members can compose these contracts at home after the first session, bring them back to the group at the second meeting, and discuss them in the group. The leader and other members can offer their perceptions of how realistic the person's goals are and can offer other ideas for ways to meet objectives.

Reading.   Depending on the kind of group, reading can be a great asset to the members. By doing some reading before the group begins, participants take time to solidify their commitment and focus. Reading can assist them in reflecting on their lives and on what they want to change. For example, for an assertiveness training group, the members can read a popular treatment that discusses typical situations in which people encounter difficulties and ways for acting in these situations in an assertive way.

Reading can be used as a focusing technique in other ways. You may be aware of a specific theme that a particular member of the group plans to explore and be able to recommend a book that helps the member focus on that topic. You may also ask members to select from among the many self-help paperbacks ones that they expect might be useful for them. Or you may give members a bibliography about groups or about probable group topics and urge them to select ones that they think might be especially meaningful at this point in their lives. You may also encourage group participants to reread a book that has had an impact on them or to reread their favorite childhood fairy tale and reflect on whether it symbolized any struggles they faced.

Writing journals.   Writing can be used as an adjunct to group preparation in several ways: Members can spend ten minutes each day recording in a journal feelings, situations, behaviors, ideas for courses of action. For example, clients who are working at being assertive and speaking out can make journal entries about the inner dialogue they have before deciding to express an idea, about times they did express an opinion (how they felt, how others reacted to them), about times they sat quietly thinking they had nothing valuable to offer (and how they felt then), and about how to change these patterns.

Members can also review certain periods of time in their lives and write about them. For example, they can get out pictures of their childhood years and other reminders of this period and then freely write in a journal whatever comes to mind. An old school picture can result in interesting associations. Writing in a free-flowing style without censoring can be of great help in getting a focus on feelings.

Members can bring their journals to the group and share a particular experience they had that resulted in problems for them. They can then explore with the group how they might have handled the situation better. In general, however, these journals are for the benefit of the members, to help them get focused for a session. Members themselves can decide what they do with the material they write.

Another way to use journals is as a preparation for encountering others in everyday life. Jenny is having a great deal of difficulty talking with her husband. She's angry with him much of the time over many of the things he does and does not do, yet she sits on this anger; she feels sad that they don't take time for each other, yet she doesn't express her sadness to him; she feels the full responsibility for rearing the children and resents him for being indifferent as a father, yet she keeps her resentment to herself. To deal with this problem Jenny can write her husband a detailed and uncensored letter pointing out all the ways she feels angry, hurt, sad, and disappointed, and expressing how she would like their life to be different. It is not necessary that she show this letter to her husband. The letter writing is a way for Jenny to clarify what she does feel and to prepare herself to work in the group. This work can then help her to be clear about what she wants to say to her husband as well as how she wants to say it. This process works in the following way: Jenny can say aloud some of what she wrote to a member in the group who role-plays her husband. Others can then express how they experience her and the impact she has on them. Aided by such feedback, Jenny may be able to hit on a constructive way of expressing her feelings to her husband in real life.

Still another technique is for members to spontaneously enter in their journals their reactions to themselves in the group:

- How do I feel about being in this group?
- How do I see people in the group? How do I see myself in it?
- What do I fear most? How might I deal with my fears in this group?
- How do I sabotage myself so that I don't get what I might from this group? How can I challenge myself when I become aware of defeating myself?
- What are some ways in which I resist? How do I avoid?

If people write down their reactions in this way, they are likely to verbalize them in the group. For instance, if members fear opening up lest others see them as being stupid, this fear prevents them from sharing their concerns. If they write about this fear and then bring it up for consideration in the group, they lessen their chances of being stopped by the fear.

Another useful technique is for people to write down their reactions to each session. A brief review of the session provides them with a running account of their experiences in the group; toward the end of the group such notes can be useful in recalling and understanding specific events.

Writing can be useful as the group progresses as well as at the outset. At the midpoint of a group, people can take time during the week to write down how they feel about the group at this point, how they feel about themselves and their participation in it so far, what they are doing outside the group to attain their goals, and how they'd feel if the group were to end now. By discussing these statements in the group, participants are challenged to reevaluate their level of commitment and are often motivated to increase their participation in the group.

Using structured questionnaires. A sentence completion questionnaire that includes the following statements might be administered to a group in an early session.

- What I most want from this group is . . . .
- The one thing I'd most want to be able to say at our last meeting is . . . .
- Thinking about being in this group for the next 20 weeks, I . . . .
- A fear I have about being a group member is . . . .
- One personal concern I would hope to bring up is . . . .
- I often feel . . . .
- The one aspect I'd most like to change about myself is . . . .
- Something I particularly like about myself is . . . .

This is a focusing device, and it can be followed with a discussion of whatever it brings out in the members.

A problem check list is another valuable tool for helping members decide how they want to use group time. For example, for an adolescent group you can develop a list of problems that adolescents typically face, and members can write down the degree to which each problem applies to them (anonymously if they wish). The inventory in the box is an illustration.

PROBLEM CHECKLIST FOR ADOLESCENT GROUP

Directions: Rate each of the following problems as they apply to you at this time and indicate the degree to which you'd like help from the group with them.

1. This is a major problem of mine, one I hope will be a topic for exploration in the group.
2. This is a problem for me at times, and I could profit from an open discussion of the matter in this group.
3. This is not a concern of mine, and I don't feel a need to explore the topic in the group.

- Feeling accepted by my peer group
- Learning how to trust others
- Getting along with my parents (or brothers, sisters, etc.)
- Getting a clear sense of what I value
- Worrying about whether I'm "normal"
- Being fearful of relating to the opposite sex
- Dealing with sexual feelings, actions, and standards of behavior
- Being too concerned about doing what is expected of me to the extent that I don't live by my own standards
- Worrying about my future
- Wondering whether I will be accepted into a college
- Trying to decide on a career

Additional problems I'd like to pursue:

```
L_____J
```

A questionnaire does not have to be this elaborate. In an adolescent group, for example, one could simply ask: "What problems would your parents like you to discuss in this group, and what would you like to say about these problems? What kind of issues might your peers suggest to you for exploration in this group?"

Constructing a critical-turning-points chart. Another technique for preparing members for productive work in groups is to ask them to draw a road map of their lives and include some of the following points of interest: major turning points, major crises, big decisions, new opportunities, major accomplishments, key failures, important people, major disappointments. Members can then work in pairs, selecting whatever they would like to share from their charts. Or members can talk about critical turning points in their lives with the entire group. In addition to or in place of a chart, people can draw a sketch divided into three parts: "My Past/My Present/My Future." Much of their drawing may be symbolic. Again they can share what parts of their sketch mean to them in small groups or in the group as a whole.

Writing an autobiography. Another technique for getting members focused is to ask them to write autobiographies in which they present their current subjective views of various points in their lives: childhood, adolescence, early adulthood. They can be encouraged to stress significant events, persistent emotions, dreams, relationships with significant persons, and parallels in their lives at present. They might pay particular attention to those events that evoked intense emotions because these may contain clues to work they decide to pursue in the group.

Using fantasy. An open-structured or nondirective fantasy technique can be useful in the early stages of a group for individual focusing, for providing data, and for getting group members acquainted with one another. One such exercise, which can be done in writing or orally, goes like this: "Imagine that you are a book. What's a good title for you that captures something of what you are all about? What's your style, your tone? What are your chapter headings? How about your cover and your preface—will people be enticed to read you, and how will they be? Are you going to deliver what you advertise? Which chapters of you were the hardest to write? Which chapters would you want to have deleted? After people have read through you, cover to cover, what do you suppose they will think?"

The same device can be used during the ending stages of a group when members are being asked to consolidate their group experience. "Thinking back to the book you imagined yourself to be at the beginning of this group, do you want now to have a different title? What other changes and revisions would you like to make, from beginning to end?"

Preparing members to get the most from a group

At the initial session you can discuss with members some guidelines for involving themselves in the group and applying what they learn in the group to their daily lives. We believe that participants need to know how groups work in order to gain the most from their participation. Of course, there is a danger in overpreparing members. By spending too much time teaching them what to look for and how to act in a group, you run the risk of doing too much of the work that the group ultimately needs to do for itself. Not every possibility should be covered; however, some preparation at the outset can create a climate conducive to productive work as the group moves into its advanced stages. All this preparation doesn't have to be completed at the initial session; much of it needs to be reinforced and discussed during the first few meetings.

The best way to distribute this information is to write it down and give it to members at the screening interview, the preliminary session, or the first group session. The list in the box is designed for growth groups for relatively well-functioning adults. It can be shortened or modified depending on the specific population.

GUIDELINES AND SUGGESTIONS FOR GROUP MEMBERS

1. *Have a focus.* Commit yourself to getting something from this group by focusing on what you hope to accomplish. In clarifying your goals, review specific issues you want to explore, specific changes you want to make, and what you are willing to do to make these changes. Prior to each group session, take time to get clear about what you would like to bring up during that meeting and write these issues down if that is helpful to you.

2. *Be flexible.* Although it helps to approach a group session with some idea of what you want to explore, don't be so committed to your agenda that you cannot work with what comes up spontaneously within the group.

3. *Don't wait to work.* It is easy to let a group session go by without getting around to what you hope to do or say. The longer you wait to actively involve yourself, the harder it will become.

4. *Be "greedy."* The success of a group depends on your being greedy to do your own work. This doesn't mean that you should monopolize time or be insensitive to the difficulty others might have in getting into the spotlight. But if you constantly wait until it's your "turn" or try to monitor how much of the group's time should be allotted to you, you inhibit the spontaneity and enthusiasm that can make a group exciting and productive. If each of you takes responsibility for pursuing your own work, everyone should have enough opportunity to take the spotlight.

5. *Pay attention to feelings.* Intellectual discussions are great, but it is not as hard to find a place for them as it is to find a place in which to talk about your feelings and convictions. That is what an experiential group is all about. If you do nothing but expound your theories and opinions, you will not explore your life on an emotional level. As a rough rule of thumb, if your sentences can just as well start "My opinion is that . . . ," you probably are not working much on a feeling level, and you are not taking full advantage of the unique opportunity for doing so that an experiential group provides.

6. *Express yourself.* Most of us are in the habit of censoring our expression of thoughts and feelings; we are afraid of being inappropriate or, often, afraid that we will simply magnify and entrench the feelings and convictions we have if we voice them. These fears are not unfounded, but we have far

more reason to be concerned about what we do to ourselves when we don't than when we do verbalize. And experientially there is a world of difference between thinking something through in our minds and saying it out loud. A group is an ideal place to find out what would happen if we expressed what we felt; this can be a powerful and positive experience. If you have feelings that relate to the group, be willing to express them. For example, if you are feeling perpetually bored, announce that you feel this way. Sitting on feelings is a sure way to dam up the flow of a group.

7. *Be an active participant.* You will help yourself most if you take an active role in the group. Silent observers are not likely to get as much from their participation in the group, and others may believe that their silence means they are being judgmental. Although silent members may be learning vicariously, they deprive others of the opportunity to learn from them.

8. *Experiment.* Look at the group as a place in which you are relatively safer and freer than usual to express yourself in different ways and to try out different sides of yourself. Having done so, you can then seek ways of carrying these new behaviors into your outside life.

9. *Grow.* Groups are built on the assumption that, no matter how well your life may be going now, it can be enriched by the opportunity to explore your feelings, values, beliefs, attitudes, thoughts, and to consider changes you may want to make. If you believe that such exploration is appropriate only for people with severe emotional problems, you shortchange yourself and the other participants. Even though you do not have any pressing crisis in your life, assume that the issues that come up for you are worth exploring.

10. *Don't expect change to be instantaneous.* If you do seek to change some features of your life, remember that such changes do not usually happen all at once or without some backsliding. Give yourself credit for what you are willing to try and for subtle changes you can see yourself making.

11. *Don't expect others to appreciate your changes.* Some people in your life may have a considerable investment in keeping you the way you are now. Expect to find less support outside the group than within it for your struggles, and use the group as a place to explore some of the resistance you encounter outside.

12. *Don't expect to be understood within the group.* Groups heighten a sense of intimacy and provide an opportunity for being understood by others in ways we don't always experience in our daily lives. But in many respects you simply will not be understood by the others in your group. They will see certain dimensions of you but will not have a good idea of what you are like elsewhere. If you are working mainly on conflicts or emotional vulnerability, the group will see this side of you. You can waste your time and everyone else's if you feel you must constantly qualify and footnote everything you express. A concern that everyone get the full pic-

ture—which probably is impossible anyway—will just distract you from achieving your goals in the group. For example, if you choose to explore some negative feelings you have about a relationship you are in and think you must explain those feelings by giving a full, "objective" account of the relationship, you will be talking forever. Better to resign yourself in advance to the idea that others won't and can't have the full picture.

13. *Don't expect to understand others in the group.* The other side of this point is that you do a disservice to others in the group if you suppose that you have them all figured out. Like you, they are presumably working on expressing sides of themselves that they do not usually have an opportunity to express. If you let yourself think that that's the whole picture, you are forgetting how complex people are.

14. *Stick with one feeling at a time.* You will have much more opportunity to learn new behavior if you immediately express yourself rather than constantly trying to put things into perspective. You can make time for that after you have said what you feel like saying. A good way to keep yourself from facing anything is to constantly stifle your expression of one sort of feeling because you are in a hurry to cancel it out with acknowledgment of a contrary feeling. You may have mixed emotions about an issue, but if you want to fully face that issue try to stick with those feelings one at a time.

15. *Avoid advising, interpreting, questioning.* As you listen to others in the group, you will often be tempted to offer advice. Doing so can occasionally be fine, but people can easily be inundated by well-meant advice. They are likely to withdraw, and you are likely to forget that you are in the group to express yourself. Your input will be much better received if it consists not of advice but of feelings and experiences of your own that the person has touched on. Similarly, when everyone starts taking on the role of the group leader in providing interpretations, the person working is likely to feel that he or she is the only one working and become defensive. People also tend to become defensive when faced with an onslaught of questions. Questions can be asked in ways that open people up rather than closing them down. As a general rule, however, you will carry your work further if you tell them your personal reactions to the issue rather than questioning them about theirs.

16. *Don't "gossip."* Here gossiping means talking about someone in the third person. Even if the person is not in the room, you get closer to what you want to say if you use "you" rather than "he" or "she." Your group leader may often encourage you to pretend that the person you want to talk about is in the room, and have you speak directly to this person. Although this exercise may seem artificial at times, it usually leads to a powerful expression of feelings or thoughts. If you doubt this result, watch how the exercise works with others in your group. Or, think of someone

toward whom you feel anger and see whether you can experience the difference by saying aloud "I'm angry with him because . . . " and then "I'm angry with you because . . . ."

17. *Don't "band-aid."* If you rush in to be helpful or supportive or comforting to someone who is expressing something painful, you are not respecting their ability and desire to fully express what they want to say. You probably know from your own experience how good it can feel to get something out instead of having it cut off by someone's ill-timed helpfulness. People grow from living through their pain; let them do it. Certainly interactions in a group leave plenty of room for words and gestures of comfort or consolation, but wait until people have gotten through their pain. Otherwise your message is that they always need a "mother" to help them.

18. *Give feedback.* When people express something that touches you, let them know by emphasizing your own feelings and reactions whether positive or negative. In the long run, your willingness to directly and honestly confront another with your reactions enhances the level of trust within the group and leads you to greater honesty in your daily life.

19. *Avoid storytelling.* If you go on at length to provide others with information about you, you wind up distracting yourself and everyone else. Avoid narratives of your history. Express what is present, or express what is past if you are presently experiencing it.

20. *Exaggerate.* You can worry too much about whether you are acting when you focus on a feeling you have. Rather than wondering whether you are exaggerating your emotions, give yourself permission to nurture them a bit and discover where they lead. Of course, you won't want to fake it, but you may get in touch with something genuine by throwing yourself into what you feel.

21. *Be open to feedback.* When others give you feedback about their reactions to your work, remember that, like you, they are there to try out new ways of expressing themselves directly. An easy mistake you can make here is to be too ready to accept their feedback as gospel or to be too quick to reject their insights by rebutting them or explaining away what they say. The most constructive approach usually is to listen and to think the feedback over until you get a grasp on what parts of it fit.

22. *Avoid sarcasm and indirect hostility.* A main goal of participants in an experiential group is to learn to express feelings, including anger, in a direct manner. If you feel angry, say so directly; do not use pot shots and sarcasm, which people often don't know how to interpret.

23. *React to group leaders.* It's normal for group members to react to group leaders with feelings borrowed from the past, from fantasy, and from reality. You can turn this reaction to advantage by making it a special point to explore and express your feelings about your group leaders.

24. *Beware of labels.* Watch out for the generalizations, summary state-

ments, and labels you use to describe yourself. For example, you may define yourself as a "loner" and an "outsider," and you may communicate through your behavior that you want people to stay away. Such behavior and self-imposed labels invite others to treat you as an outsider and thus become self-fulfilling prophecies as others latch onto what you say and insist on pigeonholing you for the duration of the group. Be ready to call others if you think they are reducing you to one dimension. And try to guard against assuming that once members have given themselves labels you are entitled to suppose forever that you've got them figured out.

25. *Discover your defenses.* You probably already have some idea about how you might sabotage your own work in a group—by rationalizing, withdrawing, denying, turning a specific criticism into a global "I'm no good." Look out for your usual defenses.

26. *Decide for yourself how much to disclose.* To find out about yourself you need to take some risks with saying more than you are comfortable saying. However, pushing yourself and participating in a context that puts you under some pressure should be distinguished from disclosing things about yourself simply because others seem to expect or need it.

27. *Carry your work outside the group.* You will be finding new ways of presenting and expressing yourself within the group. Don't let it go at that! Try them out in your everyday life with due respect for timing and with caution.

28. *Express good feelings.* Groups tend to focus on the negative sides of our experience. Generally these sides are more pressing than the positive sides; we usually do not get a chance to pursue them elsewhere; and they are more likely than positive feelings to keep a group moving. But you needn't conclude that there is an unspoken rule in the group that limits you to speaking only of problems and conflicts. Share your joys too!

29. *Take responsibility for what you accomplish.* The leaders and members of your group will no doubt be interested in drawing you out, but remember that in the last analysis what you accomplish in the group is going to be up to you.

[The list can also include matters such as the necessity for confidentiality, suggestions for reading, and guidelines for keeping a journal.]

Some group practitioners might argue that it is better not to give a list like the one in the box and to avoid teaching members group process on the grounds that members should struggle to find their own way. We do not agree. Our experience is that much floundering occurs when members are not given some idea of how best to do the work they came to the group to do. Moreover, we have seen group members who are psychologically wounded by hostility over their questioning, storytelling, and gossiping and who then become defensive and withdrawn for the remainder of the group. We think this outcome is unnecessary and unproductive and that it is not likely to occur if members have been told how best to participate in a group.

Preparing leaders and coleaders

In addition to preparing members to get the most from a group, you need to prepare yourself to be fully present in the groups you lead. If you do not devote time to preparing yourself psychologically, the group is likely to suffer. You can use many specific procedures to get yourself ready every time you approach a new group and for each session. We list here some of these techniques. In approaching a new group, you might ask yourself these questions:

- How ready do I feel for this group? Am I feeling available for people in the group?
- Do I want to do this group? How alive and enthusiastic do I feel?
- How effective am I feeling in my personal life? Am I doing in my life what I hope my members will do in their lives?
- Am I feeling professionally confident?
- Do I believe in the process of a group, or am I doing a group merely because I was told to?

In addition to preparing yourself before meeting a group for the first time, you can use at least some of the following procedures to prepare yourself for an upcoming session:

- Spend some time, if only a few minutes, in relaxation before you go into your group. Take time to reflect on what you'd like to accomplish.
- Be aware of your own thoughts and feelings so that you can use them in your work with others.
- Try for yourself some of the exercises and catalysts you will ask your group to use. Thus, if you intend to ask your group how they are seeing themselves and how they are feeling about themselves, ask yourself these same questions.
- Spend some time, perhaps at lunch or dinner, with your coleader. If you and your coleader are not attuned to one another, your work together will be disjointed. Talk about how you are feeling about yourself, about working as a team, about going into the group, and about any of the members. Do you and your coleader respect each other? Do you trust one another? Is one doing most of the work?

• Devote some time to thinking about the prior session. Where did the group leave off? How can you bridge the gap between the prior session and the upcoming one?

Concluding comments

In this chapter we've discussed preparation as a technique for promoting group effectiveness. We have emphasized preparation for the group experience through screening interviews, preliminary sessions, clarification of goals, preparation of members to get the most from a group, and leader preparation. Many problems in the working stage of a group arise because of inadequate preparation—because of lack of clarity about the nature of the group and about how best to participate in it. These problems can be avoided with adequate preparation.

QUESTIONS AND ACTIVITIES

1. In this chapter we put considerable emphasis on preparing group members. Why do you agree or disagree with our emphasis?
2. Drawing from books listed in our bibliography or other books with which you are familiar, review reasons some might give for not preparing members for a group.
3. Suppose you are working in an agency and are asked to organize a group for a particular population. How might you go about this? Discuss such matters as recruiting, screening, selecting, and preparing members. What would you say to prospective members about what you expect of them and what they may expect of you?
4. Discuss the pros and cons of heterogeneous versus homogeneous groups. When might you want a group composed of members who are alike? When would you want a group composed of diverse kinds of members?
5. What is your position regarding screening of members?
6. How might you tell someone you do not want him or her in a group? Would you provide alternatives? If so, what might these be?
7. At this point in your professional development, what kinds of groups or what kinds of populations do you regard yourself as qualified to lead? What are some groups that you might be most interested in forming and leading?
8. What specific factors would you look for in deciding to include someone in or exclude someone from a group? Discuss.
9. Do you believe that if you are licensed to conduct groups for certain populations you are necessarily qualified to do so, or that if you are not licensed you are not qualified? What are your reasons?

10. We discuss advantages of preliminary sessions. Can you think of any disadvantages or potential hazards to such sessions?

11. Suppose a member at a preliminary meeting is concerned about whether what goes on in the group will stay there. What would you say? Would you open up the topic of confidentiality for group discussion, declare your rules, or what?

12. Under what circumstances, if any, would you breach the confidentiality of your group members' disclosures? How might you explain this exception in the screening interview or in the preliminary session?

13. Assume that an adolescent asks you whether you would tell her parents about something she says in the group. How would you respond?

14. Think of a group that you would be interested in designing. Write a brief proposal for this specific group with a specific target population, and present the proposal to your class. Others in the class can give you feedback on your presentation as well as on the proposal itself.

15. Break into dyads, with one person assuming the role of a candidate for a group and the other conducting a screening interview. After about ten minutes, switch roles. Or break into triads, with the third person giving feedback. Partners should discuss how it feels to be the group leader doing the interviewing as well as the prospective participant being interviewed.

16. Write a list of ground rules that you might distribute or at least discuss with a group. Present these rules to a small group of classmates to get their reactions to your policies and to consider rules included in their lists but not in yours.

17. We make several suggestions for orienting and preparing participants for a group experience. Which of these suggestions are you inclined to accept and which do you reject? Discuss.

18. You are meeting your group for the first time and a member asks how he can get the most from this group. How might you respond?

19. Do you think it important for members to clarify their goals before entering a group? Explain. What would you do, or not do, to promote this clarification?

20. Some group leaders use written contracts that outline their expectations of members and what members can expect of them. What advantages and disadvantages do you see with this procedure? With what kind of group(s) might you use written contracts?

21. You discover that several members are talking outside the group about matters discussed in the group. What might you do?

22. What are your views about asking members to do reading or writing? If you see value in such exercises, how might you present them to your group? What would you hope they would gain? How would your answers to these questions vary with the population of the group?

23. Can you overprepare members for a group? How? What effect might overpreparation have on the group process?

24. We discuss the need for coleader preparation. What are the signs and consequences of lack of preparation?

25. Discuss your reactions to any part or all of the Guidelines and Suggestions for Group Members.

26. We suggest writing autobiographies as a technique to get members focused for a group. Write your own brief autobiography, mentioning critical turning points in your life and the effect they have on you now. You might want to share what this experience was like for you with others in class.

27. Another focusing technique we describe is to ask members to imagine they are a book. Do this exercise yourself. Again, you might want to form small groups and share this "book of you."

28. In this chapter we talk about the use of structure in groups. What are your thoughts about the balance between too much structure and not enough structure? What problems do you see with either of these extremes? Which side might you be inclined toward? Discuss.

29. How could this chapter be improved?

CHAPTER FOUR

Techniques for the Initial and Transition Stages

If a leader has done a good job in the preparation phase of a group, members are likely to come to the first session with a focus and a readiness to work that will help them during the initial stage. This stage is especially critical because during this time the group's identity is being formed. In this chapter we discuss some of the basic characteristics of a group during its initial stages, and we provide some techniques for getting the group started and for dealing with difficult members.

Physical arrangements and setting

An important initial responsibility of the group leader is to decide on the physical setting in which the group is to be held and to arrange this setting in a way that is conducive to group work. Two important considerations here are privacy and freedom from distractions. Sometimes, for example, group leaders think that meeting outside is a good idea because of the informality, but generally such a setting both lacks privacy and is a source of distractions.

Because the physical setting contributes to the climate of a group, some degree of attractiveness is necessary. If the meeting place has no windows and is poorly ventilated, if it is extremely cold, or if it is extremely uncomfortable, then attention is bound to be drawn away from exploring feelings and personal issues. In a clinical setting or the ward of an institution, the walls are usually bare, and the group room may be sterile and uninviting. Members can be encouraged to think of some imaginative ways of brightening the atmosphere, given the restraints of lack of money and a limited amount of material to work with. This technique helps members assume some responsibility for the attractiveness of their meeting site.

Seating arrangements are important. A group meeting in a room where members are physically separated by tables or where they are spread out has a different quality from a group meeting in a setting that promotes eye contact and allows for some closeness. On the one hand, when a member cannot see all the other members, when some members are in corners of the room, when some are sitting behind others, and when other physical barriers are present, psychological distance and fragmentation can be expected. On the other hand, when members are crowded together too much, closeness is forced on them. Another consideration here is that an atmosphere that is too comfortable and informal can foster inattentiveness. At times group leaders want to get rid of chairs because they are often uncomfortable. Mattresses and large, overstuffed bean bags, however, may invite a prone posture that causes members to tune out of the session and perhaps even be lulled to sleep.

While the considerations pertaining to physical arrangements may seem obvious, leaders can easily overlook such matters. We encourage leaders to experiment with physical arrangements to see whether they make a difference as to what goes on in groups.

Characteristics of the initial stage

Generally, at the first session both the members and the leaders are anxious. Leaders may wonder what the group will be like, whether they will be able to deal effectively with what comes up, and whether they will be able to bring a group of strangers together in such a way that the trust necessary for effective work will be created.

Members typically are anxious about being rejected, about revealing themselves, about meeting new people, and about being in a new situation. These general fears of members are mixed with anxiety about the specific issues they intend to explore and about whether they will be able to do so.

Members may also be resistant, especially if the group is not a voluntary one. They may be there physically but not psychologically; they may be skeptical about the value of groups or the purpose of the group; they may wonder how the group will be of use to them.

Even if members want to be in the group, they may be unaware of how to get involved. Should they wait to be invited to speak? What should they talk about? How personal should they be? How much detail should they give? How can they use the group to understand and deal with their problems? Should they behave the same in this group as they do in everyday life or should they behave differently?

Trust is a basic consideration. Members may ask themselves: Is it safe in the group for them to be themselves? Will what they say be listened to? Can they risk revealing parts of themselves that they generally keep hidden? What will people think of them if they reveal what they are really like? Do they dare share their reactions to other members of the group? If they are having negative feelings toward being in the group, is it appropriate to state these feelings openly in the group? And if they do, what kind of reaction will they get from others?

Members are also usually concerned about outcomes. Will the group make a difference to them, or will it be a waste of time? Will they find out that they are "crazy" or that there is something about themselves that they cannot stand?

Finally, during the initial stage people are developing roles within the group, forming power structures and alliances, carving out identities, testing the leader and other members, deciding whether they are included or excluded in the group, attempting to please the leader, and attempting to meet the expectations of other members.

In the sections that follow we discuss techniques for getting groups started; in using these catalysts, you might listen for the themes just listed and use them as clues in deciding how to proceed.

Techniques for getting acquainted

Introductions are one of the first items of business. Depending on the type of group, a variety of approaches can be tried.

Learning names.   One technique is to have people introduce themselves by name and say anything about themselves they would like the group to know. Before each person starts, he or she must repeat the names of all those who have introduced themselves previously. In this way members can learn each other's names in a few minutes by sheer repetition.

Introducing oneself.   Leaders can ask members to introduce themselves in different ways. For example, they might introduce themselves as the people they'd like to be at the time of their final session. This technique gets people to think about their goals; it gives others a sense of what each person hopes for from the group: and it gives all a chance to begin risking themselves. Or leaders can ask members to make a conscious effort to say something about themselves that is risky and difficult to say. This technique provides a way for members to decide at the outset how much they are willing to risk in the group.

The following list gives a few examples of other catalysts leaders can use to help members begin to get acquainted.

• "Could each of you make a brief statement concerning how it was for you to come to this first session today? What did you think about before coming here? What were you feeling? And what are you feeling now?"

• "What do you expect this group to be like for you? What do you hope it will be like? What do you fear it will be like?"

• "Let's have each of you state how you found out about this group. What were you told about the group?"

• "What do you most hope you'll learn in this group? What are you willing to do in this group to get what you want?"

• "Who knows anyone else in this group? Would you state any prior relationships any of you have?"

• "What are your greatest fears, if you have any, about being in this group?"

• "Did you want to come to this group? If so, what motivated you? If you didn't want to come here, how was it for you to be 'sent' here? Now that you are here, how is it for you?"

• "What kind of prior experience have you had in counseling or in groups? What have you gotten from any of the groups you've been in before?"

• "Who has a vested interest in your being here?"

Introducing each other.   Another technique for getting people introduced consists of asking members to pair up and in these pairs attempt to get to know as much as possible about their partners so that they can later introduce their partners to the entire group. Partners might avoid bombarding each other with probing questions; they can instead be active listeners and can share as much about themselves as they choose to. This technique gives members practice in speaking about themselves to one other person. This exercise typically takes about 20 minutes. The leader can announce when the time is half up so that partners can exchange the roles of listener and speaker. Otherwise quiet people may spend the entire 20 minutes in polite listening and say only a few words about themselves. Before the reverse introductions begin, members can tell their partners what, if anything, they do not want the group to know. As a variation, instead of introducing each other, members can state what it was like for them to listen to their partners. They can give their impressions of their partners and express their feelings toward them.

Setting a time limit.   You can give members an egg timer and ask them to state the aspects of themselves they deem significant in not more than three minutes. Members can share something of their past or focus on their current lives or express their hopes for their future. They can also share whatever they are feeling at the moment. This is a good follow-up technique to the previous one because it gives each member an opportunity for self-presentation. You can begin this process yourself in order to teach the members, through modeling, how to talk about themselves. It is best that members not react or respond during this go-around. Discussion can follow after everyone has had a turn. Anyone with strong reservations about taking part in the exercise can simply pass the timer to another person. It is good practice for you not to focus on this person at this time and interrupt the flow of the go-around.

This technique often provides you with data to keep in mind for use at a later time in this group. You can note especially how members use their allotted time. Some run over in an attempt to convey much detail about themselves, while others quickly run out of things to say and are embarrassed.

Using dyads and small groups.   To lessen members' feelings of being intimidated by a large group, you can ask them to form dyads or triads for about ten minutes and get acquainted with their partners. Then, they can find new partners for another ten minutes. Depending on the size of the group and the people in it, switches can be made between two and ten times. Or, after a number of changes, a dyad or triad can join with another dyad or triad and continue the exercise. This technique gives most of the participants at least a brief opportunity to make some contact with others and to say something about themselves. The use of various combinations of small groups is an excellent ice-breaker and a good way to begin to generate trust and interaction within the group. Eventually, you can convene the entire group and ask members to share briefly what they were experiencing in the small groups.

How much structure should these small groups be given? Generally, we favor bringing some focus to these subgroups, even though they may deviate from discussing the questions suggested. The advantage of encouraging discussion of particular issues is that the entire group can later focus on certain themes. Any of the questions we suggested in the list above (under Introducing Oneself) would be appropriate here.

The use of subgroups entails the risk of fostering permanent alliances. Therefore, you might check to be sure that the membership of subgroups changes frequently. If alliances do form within the group, you might comment on this development.

The leader's role.   Leaders should keep things moving in the initial go-arounds when people are introducing themselves, for in this way everyone has several opportunities to make statements and there is no sustained focus on a single individual. Leaders should also discourage members from asking questions, especially from asking why people feel as they do. If a question-and-answer format is established at the beginning, it can continue for the whole course of the group. To keep the focus moving from person to person, leaders often find it useful to have a number of go-arounds, asking several of the questions we suggested in the list above (under Introducing Oneself). Asking only one question at a time lessens the chances that members will feel overwhelmed.

Leaders can be actively involved in the introduction process in order to begin to establish trust. Leaders can share their feelings about starting the group, can state what they expect and hope for, can say something about their experience in leading groups, and depending on the particular group can say something about themselves personally. They can add what they gain from leading groups and what they hope to learn or experience in this group. Disclosures relating to how leaders are feeling now are often the most valuable, as such revelations model a focus on the sharing of present experiences for the members.

Techniques for creating trust

There is not a single technique or even a set of techniques that alone create trust. As we emphasized in Chapter 1, you, as the leader, are your most important technique. The kind of person you are and the ability you have to establish direct contact with others are likely to be major determinants of the level of trust in your groups. Using techniques without first establishing a good relationship with group members is likely to result in suspicion and holding back on the part of the members. Such a relationship is best established when you pay attention to the needs of individual members, respond to them in respectful ways, are appropriately self-disclosing, are willing to state your expectations openly, encourage members to talk directly to each other and do so yourself, are sensitive to the fears and anxieties of the members, and provide people with opportunities to openly state whatever they are feeling or thinking.

In the initial stage a basic task of a group is dealing with mistrust. Mistrust takes several forms. Members can mistrust themselves. They may ask themselves: "Do I trust myself enough to look at what is going on in my life?" "Am I trusting enough to express my feelings?" "Am I afraid that if I begin to feel sad or angry I will feel that way forever?" Members can also mistrust other members. They may have negative reactions to some members that contribute to their hesitation in making themselves known. Finally, members can mistrust the leader or coleader. Although some participants may naively have an automatic sense of confidence and trust in group leaders, others may have initial reactions of mistrust and cynicism because they perceive leaders as authority figures—mothers, fathers, police officers.

The issue of trust is not one that is settled once and for all. The issue is especially pressing during the initial stage of a group, but it continues to manifest itself in different forms throughout the time the group is together.

The leader's most important task in dealing with mistrust is to give people many opportunities to talk about their feelings early in the group. If work is to proceed, mistrust must be first recognized and then dealt with in the group. If it is not, a hidden agenda develops, the lack of trust is expressed in indirect ways, and the group grinds to a halt. If a basic sense of trust is not established at the outset and the group leader tries to push an agenda too soon, serious problems can be predicted: lack of enthusiasm, little energy, awkward silences.

You can recognize when a climate of trust has been created because members then express their reactions without fear of censure and being judged, are actively involved in the activities in the group, make themselves known to others in personal ways, take risks both in the group and in everyday life, focus on themselves and not on others, actively work in the group on meaningful personal issues, disclose persistent feelings of lack of trust and talk about what prevents them from trusting as fully as they might, and both support and challenge others in the group.

By contrast, when trust is lacking, participants are unwilling to initiate work, are unwilling to contribute when they are called on for their reactions, keep negative feelings to themselves or share them only with a clique or express them in indirect ways, take refuge in long-winded storytelling, hide behind intellectualizations, are deliberately vague, focus on others endlessly instead of on themselves, are excessively quiet, put more energy into "helping" others or giving others advice than into sharing their personal concerns, maintain that they do not have any problems that the group can help them with, are unwilling to deal openly with conflict or even to acknowledge the existence of conflict, and exert an excessive degree of group pressure as a way of achieving conformity to norms.

So far we have stressed the components of trust building that cannot be replaced by exercises alone. We have emphasized paying attention to the relationship that the leader is developing with members and that the members are developing with one another. Once members have been encouraged to express their lack of trust, trust building can be encouraged by using techniques that foster a sense of community. We present here a few techniques that facilitate the process of establishing trust and security within a group.

Exploring fears. The anxieties that participants have about themselves, other members, and the leader or coleader can be fruitfully explored as one way to generate trust. If these fears are kept inside the participants, they simply are magnified and continue to grow. If they are acknowledged openly, they subside or at least do not inhibit participation in the group.

To help participants explore their fears, the leader can ask them to close their eyes and imagine the worst thing that could occur to them in the group. Henry, for example, sees himself being verbally attacked by all the women in the group. Because he doesn't know how to respond, he imagines himself becoming paralyzed and crying unceasingly. After the exercise, members can share how they felt about their fantasy; if they like, they can share the fantasy and the fear itself. This technique allows members to express their fears openly instead of letting them fester inside unacknowledged. We find over and over that what causes problems in a group is not the feelings people do express but those feelings that they do not express.

Dealing with fears. As a leader you have a number of ways of working with fears once they have been identified. Let's suppose that Jill says "I'm afraid of being myself in here because people will reject me." Jill can live out this fantasy in the group by imagining each person systematically rejecting her. As she does so, she can state in a few words what each person in the group might say to her. Then, she can allow herself to see the entire group yelling at her and telling her to leave because she's so rotten. In the end she can imagine herself leaving and having the worst feelings possible. This method allows Jill to face some of her fears by exaggerating them and imagining the worst possible outcomes. Another approach is simply to let Jill talk about her fear of rejection in the group. Jill may admit that she has this fear in most social situations and so avoids new situations lest she be rejected. Another technique is to have all those in the group who share Jill's fear form an inner circle. Jill can lead the group by encouraging them to talk about the ways in which they are similar to her and about how they deal with their fear of being rejected.

Another way to deal with mistrust is to ask participants to imagine what it would take for them to feel secure enough to reveal themselves in significant ways. Some may say that they would want to know they were not alone in what they felt; others may say that they would want some assurance that they wouldn't be attacked by others; still others may add that they would need a group of people who cared and were supportive. Members can also break into subgroups to discuss what inhibits their willingness to trust; then, when the whole group reconvenes, you can ask what characteristics the group requires if a trusting climate is to come about. Giving participants time to imagine ideal circumstances in these ways builds trust.

Another trust-building exercise is to ask participants to look at each of the others in turn and ask themselves: "How is it to be in the group with this person? Am I willing to be open with this person?" Or participants can ask themselves: "Whom in this group do I feel the closest to? Whom do I feel the most distant from? Whom would it be easiest and hardest for me to get to know?" After a few minutes, you can ask whether anyone is willing to report any of their reactions. This device brings out into the open reservations that participants might have; these reactions must be openly dealt with if trust is to be established.

Physical trust-building exercises have a different flavor from the techniques we have been advocating. For example, in the blind trust walk a member is blindfolded and led for a walk by another. This exercise forces the "blind" individuals to trust their guides to keep them from stumbling. They can find it exhilarating to relinquish control and have confidence in another; and the guides often feel joy in knowing that another places trust in them. There are other exercises of this sort. In one, a person falls over backward from a standing position, relying on those gathered around to catch him or her. In another, all the members of the group gather around one member lying on the ground and together lift that individual into the air.

Although these techniques can be worthwhile, we believe they often produce a short-lived exhilaration and do not get people to talk about their feelings regarding trust. Trust develops naturally, by its own process; it cannot be manufactured by the use of structured or planned. exercise. Indeed, genuine trust develops slowly or not at all if the leader uses artificial techniques rather than facilitating the group's own struggle toward earned trust. Moreover, what members learn about trust in the group should carry over to their relationships outside the group. In our view, this learning is more likely to be bypassed by the use of trust walks and falling backward than by challenging participants to honestly share fears and resistances.

Techniques for dealing with resistance

One of the best ways of developing trust is to recognize the signs of resistance within a group and to deal with this resistance. Leaders should have respect for resistance as a natural part of group process. Resistance is not simply lack of cooperation, and all resistance is not negative. After all, to some extent it is perfectly normal to be cynical or to want to check out a situation before acting or to hold back making oneself known until it seems safe to do so. Thus, resistance is not something to be avoided or gotten around; pretending it does not exist will not make it disappear. Ignoring both obvious and subtle signs of resistance leads only to a group's becoming bogged down. Blaming the members for being stubborn and unmotivated is likely to increase their defensiveness. Blaming yourself for your ineptness does not help. Resistance can be constructively explored only by encouraging participants to state some of the factors that are keeping them from getting involved and by acknowledging these sources of their resistance.

Being sensitive to fears. An obvious source of resistance in the initial stage of a group is pushing participants too quickly to overcome the fears and anxieties that are normal in this stage. These fears can be compounded if a member volunteers extremely emotional and traumatic material early in the group's history. Leaders should be sensitive to this possibility. Instead of being hungry for drama they should patiently explore fears and resistances.

Modeling. A good technique for overcoming resistance in the initial stage is modeling by the leader. When you are experiencing resistance within a group, you can give your reactions without blaming the members. You can share how you experience the resistance and how you are affected by it, and you can invite members to say what they are experiencing. Such modeling encourages members to express their feelings and is an important and direct way of dealing with any resistance that is brewing in a group.

Working with involuntary groups. Resistance can be a special problem in groups composed of involuntary clients. Here we briefly discuss resistance as a characteristic of clients who are required to attend a group, and we describe some techniques for dealing with this resistance in a therapeutic fashion. Too often leaders assume that not much will occur in involuntary groups because members are forced to attend. This attitude is easily communicated to and picked up by the members. The opportunities for significant change in such groups should not be overlooked.

In general, people who come to a group as a condition of parole or as a part of treatment on the ward in a mental health facility or on the order of a judge are somewhat closed. They probably haven't been told much about how groups function or about what they might gain from participating in a group. Thus, they have a cynical, show-me attitude and a passive style of resisting; they say little and expect to be questioned. Such members may have some of the following thoughts and feelings:

- "I'll say as little as possible, and that way I won't give anyone any ammunition to use against me."
- "They might be able to get my body here to this group, but I'll be damned if they'll get anything out of me."
- "Why should I open up and trust these leaders? They've never been in my shoes. How could they possibly understand me?"
- "I can't see why I should let anyone in here know what I'm thinking. I've survived by being tough all my life. Why should I start to trust people now, and why should I now begin to need anybody for anything?"
- "This is just another game. I'll figure out the rules of the game, say the right things, and then maybe I'll get out quicker."
- "My big problem is that I got caught. I'll be careful from now on and just not get caught."
- "These guys leading the group are supposed to be experts, so I'll let them show me. I'll sit back and watch and make them prove themselves to me. I'll show them that whatever they have to offer won't work."

If resistant members are encouraged to verbalize these thoughts, the words they use can provide material for inventing a technique to explore the resistance further. For example, the client who uses the word *ammunition* can fantasize out loud about what other group members may "shoot" her with. The person who says that nothing will be gotten out of him may be asked to pretend that each of the other members of the group is trying to break into him, as if he were a strongbox with treasures inside, and he can then specify what each person is going to try to do to get inside him. The person who thinks the leaders have never been in her shoes can be asked to talk about what she sees in the leaders that convinces her that they will not be able to share her experiences. The person who says that talk never changes anything can be asked to identify some things that matter to him that talk is not going to change. The point is that leaders should identify the existence of resistance in a group and then work to make that resistance explicit. In doing so they train the group members to express themselves, and they help establish a climate of trust because they communicate to clients that they understand and respect their resistance and are willing to work with it rather than trying to argue it away. In a subtle way this technique bypasses resistance because members who came determined not to talk are now talking. Leaders should be careful to present the technique in language that is understandable, with a minimum of jargon.

Another potentially useful device is simply to allow the members to express openly for a time their feelings about being forced into a group, without comment from the leader and especially without the implication that they shouldn't feel that way. This technique is a good one to use at the beginning because this may be the first time that anyone has listened with respect to what these people have to say, and this respect can be the basis for building trust. Eventually the leader can begin to deal with the feelings of resentment, hostility, helplessness, and defiance by saying "Now that you have expressed these feelings, what can you do about them?" This technique leads the group beyond complaining and prevents the meeting from becoming merely a bitch session. It provides the beginning of contact and the beginning of a group.

Another technique for dealing with resistance in clients who are required to attend a group is to make brief contacts with them individually and to spend some time getting to know them. Clients, especially those who live together and attend group as a part of the treatment program, frequently have had no orientation to a group; they are merely told to attend. A brief contact or several contacts outside the group can be the beginning of rapport.

A direct technique for use in a group session is to encourage questions about how the group will function, what the leader's role will be, and related matters. Some members may assume that whatever they say will be recorded and perhaps used against them. You can help establish trust in this situation by being honest about your role in the group and about how much of what goes on in the session you will report. For example, if you are required to keep notes on clients and put a summary of their progress in a file, you can assure clients that you will discuss with them what is going into their folders. Or you can role-play what you are going to say to supervisors about clients.

A basic approach for working with involuntary groups is to inform members that, although they must attend the sessions, you are open to input from them, and they will have a significant impact on how the time is used. You can then point out some possibilities. Members who come to a group reluctant to do more than put in their time might find value in such a group if alternatives to using that time are explored. Also, members should have an opportunity to evaluate the group from the early stages. Resistance can often be lessened when members are encouraged to assume some responsibility for how the group functions.

Another freedom sometimes available to involuntary clients is not to participate in the group session. They are obliged to be there physically, but they can form an outer circle where participation is not required or allowed. If they change their minds, they can join the inner circle, which is a working group. There may be some limitations to the use of this technique: it may not be allowed by the institution, or the working members in the inner circle may object to being observed by silent members.

Techniques for dealing with defensive behaviors

In this section we give a number of examples of typical avoidance behaviors—the kinds of defenses that members often employ in the initial stage of a group. For each of these behaviors we suggest approaches and techniques for dealing with it.

Having an external focus.   Members in the initial stage of a group frequently focus on other people and on matters external to themselves. They may blame others either inside or outside the group for their inability to trust. For example, Darlene announces that she finds it difficult to be in the group because Charlie sits back and looks bored. She focuses much of her attention on what Charlie is doing, what he's not doing, and how she thinks Charlie is "making" her feel instead of looking at herself and her reactions. In this way she avoids dealing with her lack of involvement in the group. In this situation the leader might ask Darlene to speak directly to Charlie and tell him how she is affected by his presence in the group. If Darlene says "Charlie is so aggressive," the leader, assuming she is responding to Charlie the way she responds to significant figures in her life, can encourage her to replace this statement with "Charlie, you seem aggressive, and I find myself reluctant to open up around you. You remind me of my ex-boyfriend." This technique of directing the focus toward members who are making statements about others gets members to look at themselves and their part in the group.

Using impersonal and global language.   John characteristically speaks in general terms and thus keeps himself shut off from other members. When, during one of the early sessions, the leader asks members to state how they feel about being in the group, John says: "Nobody in here really wants to open up. Everyone is sitting back and waiting for the other guy to begin. People don't want to say what they think; they don't want to step on anyone's toes. Nothing is happening in here because they are all putting up walls, and nobody wants to come out from behind these walls." Because John uses universal terms such as *nobody, they,* and *everyone,* others in the group have no idea whom he is talking about. Also, it's not clear whether he is including himself in this category because he doesn't claim that he has walls or that he is not willing to open up.

The following statements, questions, and suggestions that a leader might direct to John indicate the kinds of techniques that might be useful in this situation.

• "John, what you just said is rather vague. I wonder if you'd be willing to go around the group and state how you see each person in this group so far. It might help if you describe how you see each person as having walls, and tell each person how it feels to have these walls between you."

• "I am aware that you are talking about 'them' and I'm wondering whether you see yourself as part of 'them.' I have something I'd like to suggest as a way that you might begin to initiate some openness in this group. Would you be willing to look at each of the members in this group, and, as you look at each one of us, imagine to yourself the walls that *you* might be building to keep your distance from each of us?" After a few minutes: "Are you willing to pick one person in this room and tell that person about any of the walls that are within you, and what you imagine would happen if you took your wall down?"

• "How about going around the circle and completing this sentence in a different way as you look at each person, John: 'One way I'd like you to be different in here so that I could be different is . . . .'"

• "Perhaps you'd be willing to tell us some of the ways in which the situation in this group seems like situations you find yourself in outside the group. How are you the same both in the group and in daily life?"

• "Could you replace each of the remarks you have made about other people's walls with a comment about some wall of your own?"

Asking questions of others.   A particular form of avoidance behavior that can occur during the beginning of a group is asking questions of others. This defense drains away the energy from a group. Members using this defense demand that others make themselves known, while they keep themselves safely hidden through their questions. For example, Jim perceives himself as an active and involved member merely because he bombards other members with questions. Even though the group is relatively young, Jim has already managed to ask personal questions of most of the members. He's asked others to give reasons for the feelings they have, and he's asked them whether they have tried this or that approach to solving a problem. In general his questions have interrupted group interaction.

Keeping in mind that Jim's style of questioning others is a way of avoiding focusing on himself, the leader can use either of two techniques to get Jim to make personal references. The leader might ask Jim to go around the entire group and ask every question that he might possibly want to ask of everyone in the group (members should not answer these questions). The point of this exercise is to allow Jim to exaggerate his questioning behavior. When he's finished, the leader can ask him what he is feeling and can also ask him to tell each member what he might want from him or her. Alternatively, the leader can ask Jim to refrain from asking a question and instead to talk about what in him prompts the question. In this way, Jim can begin to disclose something of himself.

Techniques for dealing with difficult members

Certain kinds of difficult members are most conspicuous in the initial stage of a group; the leader's responses to them early in the group's history are crucial, for the leader sets a tone for the group through these early interactions. In this section we discuss such participants and give suggestions for dealing with them.

The description of a member as difficult can be appropriate or it can be the result of leader countertransference. Most leaders are sometimes unsure whether their reactions to an individual are valid or are rooted in their own idiosyncracies and unresolved conflicts. In general, we assume that our personal reactions to group members genuinely tell us about them, even if they simultaneously tell us about aspects we need to explore further in ourselves. The perceptions we have of our clients are in many ways our best tools and the source of our techniques. For this reason, we allow ourselves, with some caution, to be guided by them. When others in the group share our reactions to an individual, their feedback can help us sharpen our awareness of a situation.

Because leaders have a responsibility to a whole group, they may decide to ask a difficult individual to stop coming. However, this solution can be damaging both to that individual and to the trust of the other members. The negative impact of the member on the group must be weighed against the impact of excluding him or her. Asking someone to leave the group should rarely be necessary, especially with adequate screening and preparation. Those who exhibit problematic behaviors in the group can usually be dealt with in a direct and caring manner and can be given more of a chance to change in the group than they might be given in daily life.

The greatest responsibility of leaders working with difficult members is to facilitate insight and growth, both for them and for the other members. To do so, leaders cannot rush in too quickly with ways of changing difficult members or "curing" them of their problematic behavior. Initially leaders should gather data; they should ascertain whether the difficult members see themselves as causing problems for themselves or others, and they should ascertain what the difficult members might be attempting to communicate through their behavior.

Leader modeling is extremely important here, for members do learn through this process. A common danger is to quickly sum up difficult members by attaching labels ("monopolizer," "group nurse," "seductive one"). Such labeling can encourage scapegoating, which only entrenches and solidifies these members' styles by motivating them to retreat defensively into the identity given them. A general guideline for leaders is to avoid saying "You are difficult" and to say instead "I am having difficulty with you." Leaders can then continue by pointing out specifically how and why they are being affected the way they are. For example, rather than saying "You are a storyteller, and by telling stories you are a bore," the leader might say: "When you go on in such great detail about another person, I have a hard time paying attention to you. I would much rather hear how you are affected by this person." When members know the specific behavior leaders are having difficulty with, they can learn to observe this behavior in themselves. Then they are in a position to decide whether the behavior is a problem to them and also whether they are willing to change in this respect. In the example given, the member may realize that she typically loses others by going on in such a detailed fashion, yet she might decide that she doesn't want to change this aspect of herself.

If leaders initiate feedback about a difficult member, they may check out their observations by asking others to give their reactions. If others initiate the feedback, leaders may add their own. However, they should be alert to the possibility that the individual will receive more feedback than can be assimilated at a given time, and they may intervene by saying "Perhaps John has had enough of our telling him who we think he is, and we can focus more on what's going on with each of us." Here, in order to offer a lead to further work, a leader might add "Before we do that, John, I'd like you to have an opportunity to respond to any of this feedback."

Although difficult members may experience any sort of feedback as criticism, it is nevertheless best for you, as the leader, to support the right of others to voice their reactions. However, you might also communicate strong supportive interest in and caring for the recipients of the feedback: acceptance of them, patience with them, and willingness to stay with them even though doing so is difficult. You might let difficult members know that the feedback from others is compatible with their caring for the difficult members. If you honestly can do so you might convey a willingness to accept difficult members as they are, while at the same time conveying to them the opportunity for behaving in ways that would affect you differently. Thus you can ask such members whether there is anything they would like to try doing differently or whether there is further work they would like to pursue.

We cannot give complete recipes for working with members who demonstrate difficult behaviors in a group. Your own reactions and inventiveness have to be the guide. In this regard, your abilities to be honest, sensitive, caring, and timely are of the utmost importance. It may often be inappropriate to introduce any explicit technique at all beyond encouraging feedback and individual expression and offering interpretation or comments on group process.

In considering interventions, you should remember that the group is still in its initial stage. It may be inappropriate to promote much in-depth work with a difficult member who has received confrontive feedback (although that member may proceed to do such work anyway), for even if this person is now ready to express some emotion or to work on some difficult and threatening material, the others in the group may not be ready for this work and may be excessively frightened by what they see as the consequences of giving feedback to one another. As we mentioned earlier, the initial interchanges with difficult members should be seen primarily as a source of valuable information for you to use later on. For example, you may want to ask difficult members whether the responses they elicit from the group match the responses that they get in everyday life or that they got in childhood.

Techniques for working with a difficult member fall into two categories: those that focus on the member and those that focus on the responses of others to this member. Either focus can flow into the opposite, and you should be alert to this possibility. Techniques that focus on the responding members include asking them to comment on "times I've felt before as I feel with you now," on "times I feel outside the group as I feel with you now," or on "this is how I feel with you now and these are the options I have in dealing with these feelings." Techniques that focus on the difficult members include having them receive feedback in order to clarify the impact they have on others; having them exaggerate their behavior, perhaps to see it clearly, perhaps to tire of it, or perhaps to gain insight into its sources; having them try out different behavior; and having them clarify that they are behaving as they want to behave.

During this kind of work, you need to be alert to the danger that group members will label difficult members or that these members will label themselves, particularly when they feel defensive, and then live up to these labels for the duration of the group. One of the purposes of a group is to provide a context in which participants can challenge self-defeating labels and begin to create positive identities. In this regard, techniques that invite difficult members to experiment with new forms of behavior are especially useful. In this way, members not only can think about ways in which they have embraced a limiting vision of themselves but also can learn that they do not have to live by restrictive labels.

One way of stimulating difficult members to consider changing their behavior is to ask them whether they are getting from the group the kind of experience they came to get. If there is a discrepancy between the goals they have stated and how the leaders or the group members are seeing them, they can be invited to change their course. In this way leaders can check whether the difficult members themselves want to change. Are they interested in feedback? Do they think that they may be restricting themselves by accepting self-imposed labels or the labels others have given them? Do they want to take the risks involved in creating a different identity? If they decide that their current behavior is not working for them and they want to change it, then the group is an excellent place for them to learn constructive behavior patterns.

Before suggesting specific techniques for dealing with difficult members in a group, we want to underscore our key points. Whom you experience as difficult depends on you as well as on your clients. You can trust your reactions, while also acknowledging that these assessments reflect on yourself and on your own dynamics. You can seek to communicate to difficult members your own responses to them and can thus model this kind of feedback for other group members. You might also try to communicate a basic respect for the individuals whose behaviors pose difficulties, even though the feedback given to them may be critical. Most important, you can be alert to how this kind of feedback may entrench clients in their problematic behaviors. You can communicate to these group members your openness to them as they now are as well as encourage them to consider experimenting with ways of being different as a means of obtaining the goals they stated when they came to the group.

   The person who is silent.   Leaders need to model respect for silent members if they hope to create a climate that invites rather than forces members to participate. At the same time, it is important for leaders to communicate to silent members their interest in hearing from them, and it is important that leaders be aware of the impact silent members may have on the others. In many groups other members will eventually comment on those who are silent, and those who are silent may more fully experience the interest others take in them if leaders wait for the group to initiate this feedback rather than giving it themselves. If leaders do initiate the topic of silence, they can state their hope that those who have not participated are getting what they want from the group. They can then encourage silent members to discuss what is inhibiting them. They can also inform silent members of the impact they have on others, particularly when others seem to be inhibited for fear of being judged by those who do not participate. Finally, leaders can express an interest in whether the silence of these members within the group is indicative of their styles outside group, and they can remind silent members of their opportunity to try out a different way of being.

   Both group leaders and the other participants can make the mistake of pushing the silent person to open up without discovering why the person is being silent, and they can make the mistake of focusing on the quiet member and using many means of drawing this individual out. As a result the quiet member often becomes increasingly silent, withdrawn, and resistive.

   A technique for exploring the reactions of active participants to those who are silent is to encourage them to tell one another or a silent member (depending on how threatening the leader judges this to be) how they feel about having expressed themselves around others who have not reciprocated. Exercises of this type can be introduced in a way that minimizes embarrassment to those who are typically silent; their purpose is to allow the verbally active members to work with their own feelings. Or the feedback to the silent members can be confrontive and challenge them to share more of themselves. We cannot give a blueprint for what is appropriate here. You may want to be more confrontive with someone whose silence is manifestly hostile and disruptive and more supportive with someone who is a part of the group but shy or inhibited.

   A technique for working with several silent members is to ask them to form an inner circle and then say as much as they are willing to about their being silent. The leader should be sure that these people are interested in doing the exercise.

A variation of the preceding technique focuses on the active members. They can form an inner circle and talk about how they feel left out of what the members who are silent are thinking. This exercise gives those in the inner circle an opportunity to discuss how it is for them to disclose in the presence of those who do not. It also gives those who are verbally inactive in the outer circle feedback about the impact of their silence on others.

As a further illustration of possible techniques for dealing with the member who is habitually silent, we now describe Donna and apply some of the principles we've just been discussing. When the leader asks Donna how she experiences the group so far, she shrugs her shoulders and says: "It's hard for me to talk in a group. I prefer being a listener. I don't like feeling forced to talk and to say what I think. I learn a lot just by listening to what others in here are saying." One approach here is to ask Donna whether she'd like to be different from the way she is. Would she like to be more verbal in the group? Is her listening style satisfactory to her? Is she getting what she wants by being silent in the group?

Or the leader can say: "Donna, I'd guess you don't realize how powerful an impact your silence has on me. For example, I find myself fantasizing that you don't approve of how I'm leading this group, and I wonder whether other members might tell you some of their fantasies about how you see them?"

Or the leader can ask Donna to talk about what it is like for her to be in the group. How does it feel for her to be a listener? How is her behavior characteristic of the way she is outside the group? What factors is she aware of that keep her from saying what she is thinking and feeling in the group? By answering these questions, Donna is letting people know something about her.

Donna eventually may say that she talks little in the group because she doesn't know what is expected of her; she has never been in a group before. She may say that the others seem to know what they want from the group but she still doesn't know what to work on. One technique to use here is to ask Donna to look at each person in the group and complete the sentence "When I look at you, I think that you expect me to . . . ." She may add, for example, ". . . talk as much as you do," ". . . tell some deep secret that is within me so that you can know me," ". . . come up with some problem to work on in this group," ". . . become involved in this group or decide to leave," ". . . tell you that

I am not judging you and that I accept what you are saying," " . . . show some feelings," ". . . tell you something about myself." Donna's statements provide rich material for the leader to tap into. To check the accuracy of her expectations, Donna can then ask each member what he or she does expect of her.

Another technique for working with expectations is to focus on Donna's expectations of others. She can go around the group and complete the sentence "Looking at you now, I expect you to . . . ." These two exercises can be combined by asking Donna first to go around the group stating what each person expects of her and then to go around making statements about what she expects of each person.

A final suggestion for working with a silent member like Donna is to ask her to close her eyes and imagine that the way that she has begun the group—namely, assuming the role of listener—is the way that she will continue until the end of the group. Donna can be directed to imagine that this is the last session. What is she thinking now? What has she gotten from the group? How does she feel about her level of participation in the group? What might she be saying to herself? This technique is designed to get Donna to think about the pattern of behavior she is developing in the group and to project this pattern into the future. It gives her a chance to examine how she may be allowing expectations that she imagines others have of her to interfere with her participation in the group, and it gives her a chance to declare what she would be willing to do differently if she doesn't like what she sees when she closes her eyes.

The person who monopolizes.   Although the member who is silent is likely to be challenged by the group, the person who monopolizes group time is often less likely to be effectively challenged. Some leaders prefer to let group members struggle with a monopolizer in their own way. If you prefer having a group in which many take an active role, however, you may choose to intervene. Here again a technique may not be called for; sharing your observations and reactions may suffice. Techniques that draw out the reactions of others are appropriate here because those who monopolize are already getting plenty of time. You should guide this feedback to guard against inhibiting the talkative individuals too much. You should communicate that those who have spoken so often are valued for what they have said, and you hope that they will continue to be active while others become active as well. A powerful technique to use with persons who monopolize, as well as with other difficult members, is to videotape or tape-record their work. By providing direct feedback, the tapes allow these members to evaluate how they present themselves. In addition, highly structured techniques such as using a stop watch or an egg timer, may be appropriate to limit the participation of individuals who take up too much time.

Another technique that may be useful with monopolizing individuals and with other difficult members is to recommend that they persist in their behavior. Thus, by saying "I'd be interested in seeing what would happen if you talked *more* often," you can often challenge these members to talk less. You can then comment on this response and explore it.

Often a difficult client is able to assimilate feedback that is given caringly but humorously. A leader can, for example, urge other members to give to them imitations of how a monopolizer appears to them.

The person who is sarcastic. Clients are not challenged to deal with their feelings as long as they continue to express them indirectly. Voicing anger directly is constructive, but expressing anger in a disguised form through sarcasm is not. Jan says "I'm not as high class as Marie, but I dress nicely." Jan is probably indirectly saying that Marie is snooty, but Jan isn't facing her hostility toward Marie, and Marie feels vaguely affronted by Jan without knowing exactly what she has been told. If this sarcasm is a persistent trait of Jan's, it can poison the trust and sharing of the group. In addition to eliciting feedback and responses from other group members here, such as asking Marie what she thinks Jan has just told her, you might want to introduce techniques to teach Jan directly how she can straightforwardly express the anger she evidently feels. A different approach is to ask Jan to make a sarcastic remark to every member of the group and then to comment on how it was sarcastic and what it indirectly revealed about herself. If she is ready for in-depth work, you can introduce a technique that explores whom she learned her sarcastic style from and why she needs to disguise her anger.

The person who always focuses on others. Individuals who do not give of and focus on themselves often cause difficulty in a group. This category includes self-appointed group leaders, those who seek to bandage the pain of others without allowing them to explore it, those who constantly offer advice, those who question others endlessly, those who assert that they no longer have the problems others are struggling with, and those who bestow the pearls of wisdom they have gleaned from their experience. All these members tend to give the impression that they no longer have any struggles of their own, thus providing a less than supportive environment for those who seek to be open about their problems.

Like the silent members, these members are likely to be challenged by others in the group. It is a good idea for the leader to encourage other members who are feeling inhibited to express and work with their reactions. This feedback in itself is often all that is needed to cause the difficult members to focus on themselves. In addition, leaders can teach group members that, paradoxically, we sometimes give more to others when we let others profit from the time we take for ourselves than when we direct our attention to trying to help them directly.

These techniques are not intended to take away from members a sense of altruism or a desire to help others but to show them that the group is seeing only one side of them: their need to give advice, to give comfort, or to take care of others. The goal is for such members eventually to see the group as a place where they can get something for themselves, where they can learn to receive from others, and where they can decide whether their giving style is working for them or whether they might not profit from adding other dimensions to themselves.

One technique for encouraging change is to ask the kind of member being described to go around and give each person one piece of advice and then say "And from you I want . . . ." This technique allows the person to do what comes easily, to give advice; it also asks the person to do something difficult, to ask for something from each person. Of course, this technique works only when the member wants to at least consider changing the type of behavior being described.

Techniques for starting a session

We have talked at length about starting groups, but we want to also give some attention to starting a particular session. Leaders may expect that group members will arrive ready to begin work, but it's generally helpful for leaders to spend a few minutes asking people to get "present" and focused and sometimes seeking to establish bridges with work left unfinished at a previous session. In a typical go-around members declare what they want from this session and whether they wish to discuss anything left over from the last meeting. Leaders might ask people who disclosed important material at the previous session whether they have further thoughts about it. This technique provides an opportunity for linking sessions and for following up on clients.

The following remarks indicate other ways of getting a group focused.

- "What do you most want from today's session?"
- "I'd like to have a go-around in which each person completes the sentence 'Right now I am feeling . . . .' "

- "Close your eyes, realize that the next two hours are set aside for you, and ask yourself what you want and what you are willing to do to get this."
- "Last week we left off with . . . ."
- "Do any of you have thoughts about last week's session or any unfinished business from then that you want to bring up now?"
- "How would you like for this session to be different from the previous one?"
- "Have you thought about anything that you talked about at the last session?"
- "When you think about this group and how it has been for you, are there any aspects that you would like to change?"

If a client's work has been cut off either because the group ran out of time or because the client was distracted and lost momentum, the leader can return to that work and take it further. It is often possible to recapture the theme and the feeling even when the client believes the opportunity has been lost. The leader can ask the client to start in again at the point where the interruption occurred, perhaps prompting with specific phrases. Without forcing the issue, leaders frequently find that the feelings return readily enough if the client will only begin speaking. If the client is strongly opposed to trying, the leader may expect that the client's pressing feelings now are about being interrupted. ("This is how it always goes. I'm always being interrupted and put on hold.") By exploring this material the client can clear the air for returning to the earlier theme. With luck this connection may just emerge automatically; the client may discover that feelings about being bypassed fit into the feelings worked on earlier.

Techniques for dealing with conflict and the transition stage

A transitional stage characterized by conflict and the expression of negative feelings is typical in the development of a group. The initial business of getting acquainted, establishing trust, and breaking down resistances and defenses gives way to testing the water by expressing negative feelings. Members challenge other members, and members challenge the leader.

Conflict is related to the issue of difficult members because many conflicts result from the failure to deal directly with these members. Also, the presence of difficult members in a group often escalates conflict. If a group is to progress, this conflict must be recognized and dealt with openly.

Intermember conflicts.   The following comments characterize the transition stage:

- "I feel that Fred is intimidating."
- "I don't like all this hostility."
- "Why do we focus so much on the negative?"
- "Some people are monopolizing the group time."
- "There's a lot of intellectualizing going on."
- "I don't belong here because my problems are not as severe as those of everyone else."
- "I'm bored."
- "We're not talking about real issues."
- "Some people sound like they have it all together."
- "I have a hard time opening up around Jim because he reminds me of my boyfriend."
- "George is slouching and looks bored."

These remarks are, for the most part, indirect, focused away from the speaker, and negative. The response to virtually all these statements might encourage two changes:(1) Change indirect confrontation to direct confrontation. Encourage the speaker to replace "some people," "he" and "she" with "John, you . . . ." (2) Place the focus with the speaker not with the other members. Encourage Sally to tell John about herself and how she responds to him rather than telling John how he is or who he is.

The group must experience and work through this stage rather than retreating to insincere politeness, but how conflicts at this stage are handled is extremely important. A group often finds a scapegoat and directs excessive and unconstructive negative feedback to that individual. One technique here is for leaders to direct attention away from the scapegoat by giving feedback to the group as a whole— describing the nature and stage of the group process as they see it and commenting on the importance of struggling with the emerging conflict in an honest way. Here are some other techniques for dealing with conflict.

- "Please state what you were thinking and feeling prior to saying that you felt bored."
- "Please sit directly in front of John. Tell him how you feel in his presence." After some time: "Now would you be willing to tell John about experiences you have had with persons in your life that your experience with John reminds you of?"

- "Would you pretend for a moment that you are George? Slouch the way he is, and talk about your fantasy of what he feels and thinks as if you were in his place."
- "Would you like to say how it feels to be told you are intimidating, Fred?"
- "You claim not to belong in the group, Ann, because your problems are less severe than those of the others. Please tell each member of the group how you differ from him or her. Afterward we will invite them to express their feelings about what you have said."
- "I wonder whether one of your parents was especially critical, Sally. If so, would you assume the role of that parent and continue with your criticisms of John?"

In the last example the leader response is fairly interpretive and is inappropriate unless the surrounding context is right. Furthermore, this intervention tends to take the focus away from the conflict in the room. It could be appropriate at this stage, however, since it could lead group members to look at and to explore their individual dynamics when expressing their reactions to others. Also it clearly is fitting to ask a client to elaborate on associations if the client has already indicated that this connection exists ("Jim reminds me of my boyfriend").

In general, leaders should check out the reactions of the person receiving the criticism but work primarily with the person giving it, partly to teach members that they are in a group primarily to explore and express themselves rather than to change others. What a leader models at this point can enhance the group's progress. A leader can demonstrate the difference between "telling John who you think he is" and "telling John how you feel in response to him."

In addition, the leader can give John an opportunity to state how he feels about what he has been told. If he seems resistant to this feedback, the leader can emphasize that she hopes he will consider what was said but that he need not accept it. She would want to be alert to the group's haranguing him or trying to force their feedback on him and could comment that the group members have found a scapegoat rather than keeping the focus on themselves. If, however, John gives his permission for further work and is interested in exploring the validity of the feedback, the leader could encourage him to talk about how it is to be the sort of person others have suggested he is. For example, if John has been told that others experience him as judgmental, and John agrees that others often see him this way or that indeed he is this way, the leader can ask him to exaggerate this characteristic by talking to the group in a judgmental manner.

Ann, who believed she didn't belong in the group because her problems weren't as severe as everyone else's, did focus on herself, but such remarks often turn out to be a disguised way of talking about others: "I don't belong here, but you folks do; you are all sick." Here you might first encourage Ann to go ahead and talk about the others—that is what is going on anyway—and then bring the focus back, more honestly, to Ann. For example, Ann may be terribly afraid of having problems like those of others in the group; once this feeling becomes evident, you would want to explore this fear and related fears concerning what might happen if Ann allowed herself to look at conflicts in her life that she habitually glosses over.

Conflicts with the leader.   A key stage in the development of the group is the challenge to the leader. How this challenge is dealt with is crucial to the future of the group. If leaders are excessively defensive and refuse to acknowledge criticism, they inhibit the members from confronting each other, with a resulting deleterious effect on the level of trust within the group. In essence, such leaders have established a double standard—one set of norms for intermember confrontation and another set for leader confrontation.

Challenges to leaders are rarely without some foundation in reality. Even though there may be symbolic value or an element of transference in such feedback, at this juncture it may be best for leaders to take the feedback at face value. Leaders who are too quick to interpret such feedback as projection or transference run the risk of closing off the critical member and teaching the group to be excessively cautious about confronting. The ultimate goal, of course, is that members learn that their reactions to others can teach them a great deal about themselves and their history, but at this stage they should simply be encouraged to trust their feelings enough to express them. The leader may want to make a mental note to return at some other time to the possible historical context of the feedback.

Leaders can expect to receive some accurate perceptions both of their role as leaders ("When Mary Ellen cried this morning, you left her hanging." "Why do you let all this attacking go on?") and of their personal characteristics ("You are cold and distant." "You're very authoritarian."). With respect to their role, they need not excessively apologize for it or defend it. They may want to say without arrogance or hostility that their role as they see it is different from what members may expect. With respect to personal characteristics, they may want to open the issue up to the rest of the group. This is an opportunity to model self-disclosure and willingness to listen to feedback. Leaders should not abdicate their leadership responsibilities by making token disclosures, by insisting that they are "just another member," or by embarking on an endless analysis of their characters.

Techniques for member self-evaluation

Early in the course of a group during the initial or transition stage, members should evaluate their participation. The leader might ask: "How do you see yourself in this group up to this time, and how do you feel about the way you are?" "If you continue being pretty much the same kind of member that you've been so far, how do you think you will feel at the final session?" "In what ways have you seen yourself as avoiding in this group so far, and what are you willing to do about this avoidance?" "What would you most like to change about the way you are or the way you feel in this group?" "How have you been for the group so far?"

Asking these questions and asking members to imagine that it is the final session and that they have continued with the style of participation they have established at this early stage of group are excellent catalysts for focusing members on the direction in which they see themselves moving. They invite members to change some of the ways that they have involved or not involved themselves in the group.

If participants state that they are dissatisfied with their participation and yet do not seem willing to do anything differently, the leader can ask them why they are remaining in the group. If they are required to attend group meetings, the leader can ask them to examine what potential benefit to themselves they may be missing if they remain as they are. This approach encourages members to look at their own roles in the group instead of waiting for others to make the first move.

What about those whose participation has been minimal? Understandably, most group leaders would like to have all the members of the group fully participate. Because of this desire, leaders at times force the issue. For example, some call on members and ask them what they think about the topic being discussed. Others ask each person in the group to answer a question. If leaders use these methods often, members may simply wait to be called on before they respond. If nothing seems to be happening, a far better technique is to address this issue directly in the group.

Leaders who are dissatisfied with the level of participation may also use structured techniques to keep things moving or to generate some activity. Use of these techniques can easily boomerang and contribute instead to the passivity of the participants, who begin to think that it is the leaders' responsibility to keep things moving. The best technique here is to help members face those times when they are not involved and to challenge them to decide what they are willing to do for themselves.

A good technique for minimizing the possibility that group members will continue in nonproductive patterns is to have them evaluate their participation and progress in a group ongoingly, perhaps by using a written form. The first time members can make this evaluation is during the initial or transition stage, and they can make it several times again during the life of the group. The member self-assessment form in the box can be used for this evaluation. (An evaluation form designed for the end of a group is described in Chapter 6.)

GROUP MEMBER SELF-ASSESSMENT FORM

Rate yourself on the following statements using a scale from 1 to 5, with 1 being "almost never true of me" and 5 being "almost always true of me" as a group participant.

1. I am an active and contributing member in my group.
2. I am willing to become personally involved in this group and share current issues in my life.
3. I see myself as willing to experiment with new behaviors in this group.
4. I make an effort to express my feelings as they come up.
5. I spend some time before a group session getting ready and some time afterward reflecting on my participation.
6. I make an effort to confront others directly with my reactions to them.
7. I continually seek to become clear about my goals in this group.
8. I listen attentively to others, and I respond to them directly.
9. I share my perceptions of others by giving them feedback on how I see them and how I am affected by them.
10. I serve as a positive model to others in the group.
11. I am willing to get involved in various exercises in the group.
12. I generally want to attend the group sessions.
13. I am able to provide support to others without coming to their rescue.
14. I take an active role in creating trust in the group.
15. I am open to considering feedback in a nondefensive way.
16. I seek to carry lessons learned in the group into my outside life.
17. I pay attention to my reactions to the group leaders and state what they are.

18. I avoid labeling myself and others in the group.
19. I avoid questioning others and giving others advice in the group.
20. I take responsibility for what I am or am not getting from the group.

When we use a self-assessment device such as that in the box, we discuss with the group the reactions of members to specific items on the form, paying particular attention to patterns and trends in the group.

Techniques for leader self-evaluation

In addition to asking members to assess their progress in the group during the initial or transition stage, leaders and coleaders can evaluate their own effectiveness in the group at this time. The form in the box can be used at different times during the life of a group for self-assessment and also as a springboard for fruitful discussions between leader and coleader.

LEADER SELF-ASSESSMENT FORM

Rate yourself on the following statements using a scale from 1 to 5, with 1 being "almost never true of me" and 5 being "almost always true of me" as a group leader.

1. I am generally enthusiastic about meeting my group.
2. I am willing to express my reactions to what is going on in the group.
3. I am able to help members clarify their goals and take steps in reaching them.
4. I am able to understand members and to communicate this understanding to them.
5. I can challenge members in a direct way without increasing their defensiveness.
6. I am able to model desired behaviors in the group.
7. I am willing to take risks in pursuing hunches I have in working with members.
8. My timing of techniques is usually appropriate in that it does not interrupt the client's work.
9. I am sensitive to picking up the client's lead and following the client rather than pushing the client.
10. I am able to challenge my initial assumptions and perceptions regarding members.

11. My behavior in the group indicates that I have a basic respect for the group members.
12. I am able to link the work of one member with the work of other members by picking up common themes.
13. I give thought to what I want to accomplish before I enter a session.
14. I allow adequate time for a summary and integration at the end of each session.
15. I am able to intervene effectively without attacking members who engage in counterproductive behavior.
16. I provide support and positive reinforcement to members at appropriate times.
17. I work effectively with my coleader, and when I don't I am willing to admit it.
18. I make use of appropriate and timely self-disclosure.
19. I use techniques appropriately and not as a way to avoid uncomfortable moments.
20. I give thought to the techniques that I use in a group and have some rationale for using them.

Concluding comments

During the initial and transition stages of a group, the following are key tasks for the leader: to create an environment that helps build trust; to deal with members' fears, anxieties, and expectations; to be aware of negative feelings and conflict within the group; to point out the value of recognizing and dealing with intermember conflict; to model non-defensive behavior when challenged; to work toward decreasing the dependence of members on the leader and increasing individual responsibility; to teach members directness and how to confront effectively; to encourage members to express persistent feelings and reactions as they pertain to the group; to help members go further in expressing personal reactions than they typically do.

QUESTIONS AND ACTIVITIES

1. How would you describe the characteristics of groups with which you are familiar in their initial stage? What kinds of techniques are you likely to use during the beginning of a group? What are your reasons for introducing these techniques?

2. Describe circumstances under which you think icebreaker or get-acquainted techniques are in order. Describe techniques you might use to help members get acquainted, and give your reasons for introducing them. What potential disadvantages are there to using them?

3. Anxiety is typically present at the start of a group. Explain your rationale for being drawn to techniques that escalate this anxiety, dissipate it, or explore it. What considerations do you think are important in your response to anxiety?

4. Examine the room you are in right now. How might you best use this room for a group meeting? What are its liabilities, and how could you maximize its potential as a group setting? What objects in the room might serve as props for techniques? Try moving objects around, and try different seating arrangements. Discuss how these changes might affect the group.

5. How does the body posture of members influence others in a group?

6. We have stated that structure is more appropriate in the initial stage of a group than later on. Do you agree?

7. Describe several techniques for use in the initial stage other than the ones we mention in this chapter. When do you think it might be appropriate to introduce these and when might it be counter-productive?

8. What are some possible dangers or disadvantages in the use of trust exercises?

9. When in a group would you engage in different types of trust exercises if at all? Explain.

10. Are you inclined to urge group members to make some declaration of what they want from the group during the early stages? What advantages or disadvantages do you see, and what techniques do you think you might employ in this regard?

11. In the early stages of a group, do you favor using some structured exercises, or do you lean more to letting a group find its own way? Discuss.

12. You are asked to lead an involuntary group. Describe how you would deal with the issues you imagine would surface in the group, and discuss what techniques might be appropriate or inappropriate for dealing with these issues. How would you attempt to explain to the members the potential value of the group?

13. Enumerate several characteristics of resistance and the possible dynamics behind these, and create techniques that you think might be appropriate for working with them.

14. Would it be a goal of yours, ideally, to eliminate all resistance in a group? Is this possible? Explain your position.

15. How would you work with a member who rejects all attempts to work through resistance? How would your strategy be influenced by whether the group was voluntary or involuntary?

16. Imagine you are a member of a group. What behaviors of yours would constitute resistance? In what specific ways would you resist? What sorts of techniques would be especially effective or ineffective in encouraging you to work through your resistance?

17. What are some of your thoughts about questioning as a technique? What difference do you see between closed questions and open questions?

18. Your group members incessantly question one another. What type of technique could you introduce here?

19. Several members of a group you are leading are imposing self-limiting labels ("monopolizer," "fragile one," "group nurse") at the outset of the group. How might you intervene?

20. What criteria can you use to determine whether a group member whom you consider difficult is actually behaving counterproductively in the group or whether this member is evoking some of your unresolved personal issues?

21. What kinds of general guidelines can you come up with for dealing effectively with group members who exhibit problematic behaviors?

22. You have a group member who draws attention to himself in numerous ways. He uses attention-getting behavior whenever the focus is not on him for any length of time, and when attention does center on him he talks at length, boring or irritating others in the group. Can you think of any techniques you might use in such a situation?

23. Fred is typically sarcastic and hostile. He stops the work of others with his indirect remarks. You sense that the trust level is being lowered by Fred's manner of venting his anger. How would you handle this situation? What might you do about the other members' reactions to him?

24. Sandy typically tells others how they should be, and she is quick to provide solutions to others' problems. While aborting their work, she also keeps the focus off herself. Can you think of any techniques that you might use in this situation?

25. Look over the list of difficult members in this chapter and think of others whom you might find difficult. Which one pattern of problem behavior do you think you would have the most trouble with

in a group you were leading? Speculate as to the personal dynamics that might be involved in your reactions to this behavior.

26. Some form of conflict and struggle for power is inevitable in a group. What are your views on this struggle, and how do you think techniques can be used in working with conflict? Do you think that conflict can have therapeutic value in a group? Explain.

27. In the first meeting of a group, a member declares that you do not have the experience or ability to be leading. How might you deal with this challenge? Would you be inclined to introduce a technique at this point, and if so what might it be?

28. In a group you are leading, a considerable amount of intermember conflict is expressed in several sessions. Finally, a timid and quiet man says to you: "Why are you allowing all this conflict and bickering to take place? What good is all of this doing anybody?" What might you say, and where might you be inclined to go from here?

29. What techniques can you think of to get members focused at the beginning of each session?

30. How would you go about evaluating your own effectiveness as a leader? Describe some specific procedures.

CHAPTER FIVE

Techniques for the Working Stage

In this chapter we concentrate on key phrases or sentences that a client might introduce during the working stage of a group, and we indicate how we might work with these statements. In these examples we assume that the sentence sums up or especially fits the particular client. We are not saying that the sentences we discuss here will necessarily arise in a group nor that they will always seem important or that there is only one way to proceed with a given sentence; different leaders might work quite differently with the sample sentences we discuss.

These sentences are generally not ones that might strike a counselor as profound or promising, and yet, given the context of work in progress with a given individual, they can be excellent springboards for introducing techniques in pursuing a hunch about what might be important to the client. The phrases a leader picks up on often reflect the leader's energy and interests as well as the client's. What we try to do here is to provide a feeling for the kinds of sentences that can be used as an occasion for creating or introducing a technique.

We may not know exactly where a phrase will lead, although we may have hunches about possible directions. As often as not, an exercise may develop in an unanticipated direction. The objective is to find ways of bringing issues and feelings into focus, and the sentences we discuss here have promise of helping to achieve this objective.

We want to emphasize again that leaders must be willing to abandon a technique and follow whatever material seems to be immediate. We introduce techniques, but clients tell us what direction to pursue. We rarely enter a group with a set idea of the techniques we are going to use. We invent these techniques during the session, basing them on promising clues and introducing them in such a way as to gracefully and quickly lead a client into the exercise. When a client is already showing some emotion, it obviously is distracting to spend a great deal of time setting up a technique. This sensitivity and spontaneity must be acquired through practice and supervision and cannot be taught in a book such as this.

An underlying rationale for most of the techniques we suggest is that it is not the leader's role to make people feel good or to solve their problems. People must work out for themselves the solutions to issues they struggle with. But the leader can provide a setting in which, through intensifying thoughts and feelings and sorting them out, clients are in a better position than they were previously to make changes. People are cut off from examining their lives by quick reassurance and advice, but they are not encouraged to do so when a leader is willing to listen and shows respect for emotions and ideas. Techniques can work simultaneously to intensify experiences and to generate information about the scope of the issue. They can provide clients with the opportunity to express their concerns (an opportunity they may be deprived of in everyday life) and with an opportunity for discovering connections with present and past experiences in their lives.

It is best that you be alert to opportunities for bringing other group members into the work of an individual client. Often part of the reason for picking a specific sentence to use in generating a technique is that it seems a promising avenue for including other group members.

The sample sentences we discuss in this chapter often arise during the working stage of a group, although they could come up at any point. A characteristic of this stage is that participants are usually, although not always, eager to initiate work or bring up themes they want to explore. During this stage the group leader may begin a session with a simple "Who wants to work?" and find that several members declare that they want some time.

This stage is also characterized by a here-and-now focus. People have learned to talk about what they are currently feeling and to talk about dimensions of their experience that are presently important to them. Hence, the work that is done typically has a direct quality, rather than seeming like detached storytelling.

Members are also willing to have direct and meaningful interactions with one another, including confrontations. Conflict in the group is recognized, and members have learned that they need not run away from it. Members are not likely to suppress their feelings of conflict with one another simply because this conflict is not always immediately resolved.

Other characteristics differentiate the working stage from the initial stage. Members more readily identify their goals and concerns, and they have learned to take responsibility for them. They are less confused about what the group and the leaders expect of them. Most of the participants feel included in the group. Those who are not active at least know they are invited to participate, and their lack of participation does not stop the work of the rest of the group. Participants trust the leader's input, interpretations, and suggestions and are less cautious about going along with the leader's suggested techniques. Communication in the group is characterized by a free give-and-take among the members and a tendency for members to engage in direct exchanges with less communicating by way of the leader. In many ways, the group has almost become an orchestra in that individual members listen to each other and do productive work together. Members may still look to the leader, in much the same way that individual musicians look to the conductor, for cues.

Members are also more in touch with themselves. They trust themselves more and are more ready to speak their minds, to experiment with different behaviors, and to push themselves to explore personal issues that they find frightening. They are hopeful about the potential for meaningful gain from their participation, and they take more responsibility not only for what goes on within the group but for carrying what they are learning into their outside lives. They commonly engage in work involving the expression of intense emotion and are not as frightened by it because they have had a chance to see such emotions expressed in constructive ways. They are less concerned about whether they will be accepted for what they say, having seen the group accept people who have shared hidden parts of themselves. Self-disclosure is the norm and is seen as appropriate. There is less game playing and less testing. The members are willing to try to integrate feeling, thinking, and behaving in their everyday situations. Issues of transference between members and the leader more readily come out in the open, and members are used to seeing how this transference can teach them about their past and present experience outside group.

During the working stage intermember exchanges are characterized by a giving and receiving of honest, direct, caring, and useful feedback. Members gain knowledge of how their behavior affects others from the ongoing feedback they receive. They tend to be more trusting of the feedback and suggestions they receive from other members, for they now know that people who give them feedback are also willing to receive it.

Group cohesion is increased during the working phase. The members have worked together to develop a trusting community, and they respect and care for each other. This sense of community encourages members to explore themselves on a deeper level than is typically true in the beginning stages of the group.

Not all groups reach the stage that we are describing. The fact that they do not does not necessarily mean that the leader is ineffective. Other factors can influence groups not to go beyond the initial stage. Variable membership in a group can inhibit attaining the working stage. Some populations simply may never be ready for the level of intensity we describe here. For example, the participants may simply be showing up and putting in time in the group because they are expected to attend. In addition, if the initial stage is poorly done, the working stage may never be reached. Some groups don't get beyond the unspoken conflicts or fears that inhibited them in their first sessions. The members may be unwilling to give of themselves beyond what is necessary for superficial encounters. They may have collectively decided to stop at a safe and supportive level of interaction rather than challenge each other to move into unknown territory. Early interchanges between members and the leader or among the members may have been characterized by harsh and uncaring words or actions. The resulting climate of distrust does not encourage members to take the risks necessary to move to a deeper level of interaction. The group may see itself as a problem-solving group—one that discourages full expression of thoughts, beliefs, feelings, attitudes, and experiences. This problem-solving orientation tends to cut off self-exploration, for as soon as a member raises a problem, the other members attempt to look for immediate answers. For these reasons and others some groups never progress beyond the initial stage.

When a group does get to the working stage, it doesn't progress as neatly and tidily as our characterization may suggest. As our comments on the sample sentences that follow show, earlier themes of trust, unconstructive conflict, and reluctance to participate surface again and again. Trust is not a matter that is dealt with once and for all during the initial stage of a group; as the group faces new challenges, deeper levels of trust have to be earned. Also, considerable conflict may be resolved in the initial stage, but new conflicts emerge and must be faced. In a sense, a group is like any intimate relationship: it is not static, utopia is never reached, smooth waters may turn into stormy waters for a time, and commitment is necessary to do the difficult yet rewarding work of moving forward.

We have identified traits we see as generally present in a group's working stage. This is the context for the specific situations to which we now turn. We have grouped these situations under the themes they portray. The same statement may often indicate more than one theme and therefore the possibility for more than one kind of response. In these cases, the statement is discussed under more than one heading.

Working with fears and resistance

"What if you don't like me?" Group members are likely to feel that they will not be liked if they are open with their thoughts and feelings. Laura is a member of a group that is to meet for seven daylong sessions. In the middle of the third meeting, some of the members tell her that, although she has participated, they do not think she has shared much of herself. Laura replies that she's afraid that if she says more she won't be liked. Another member, Ruth, observes that at times Laura seems to be looking on disapprovingly when other members reveal something about themselves, and as a result she feels Laura may not like the rest of the group. Laura says that she does indeed find herself thinking critically about other people.

Here the leader can ask Laura to voice some of her reactions to each of the members of the group and encourage her to include critical comments. In every instance Laura's remarks may be critical of the person to whom they are directed, but Laura may also display much insight and genuine caring. Laura can thus discover that her criticalness is appreciated and is constructive without being devastating. This outcome often occurs when people such as Laura voice the critical thoughts they are so frightened of. Ruth's feedback to Laura is helpful, but the leader may be struck by the fact that Ruth also seems to convey an attitude of disapproval. This is a good opportunity to pursue work with both individuals at once. The leader can ask Ruth to give an imitation of how she sees Laura and then invite Laura to give an imitation of Ruth. Imitations and mimicry can be effective techniques for giving and getting feedback, and they often provide an element of humor that makes the feedback memorable and easy to accept.

Perhaps this is a good point to comment on humor in groups. When we first were conducting groups, we worried that if there was much laughter nothing important was being accomplished. But we have come to think that even if laughter sometimes indicates avoidance it is just as often a powerful vehicle for important therapeutic work. People are often at their most insightful when they are able to laugh. In fact, sometimes we introduce techniques designed to generate laughter. Yet promoting humor in a group can be as much a tactical error as trying to avoid it. What works best is the humor that is a natural outgrowth of group process; here, as almost always, the role of the leader is to follow the flow of the group and invent ways to amplify that process.

"There's someone here I don't like."   Hostility is indicated when one member of a group is unwilling to work with another. In a workshop we conducted, a participant, John, announced that there was one person whom he did not want to be in a subgroup with. We made a tactical error by not doing more with John's remark and paid for it later because the group was especially slow to develop trust and cohesion. Since John did not say specifically whom he disliked, everyone else was left to wonder. Wisely or not, we were not willing to directly confront John at the time because we sensed that this particular group might perceive us as authoritarian if we insisted that John specify whom he disliked.

A technique that could have cleared the air without subjecting anyone to devastating confrontation would have been to ask the group members to share their fantasies about whether they saw themselves as the person John didn't want to be with. This technique would have allowed all members of the group to acknowledge and work with the reactions that several of them probably had to what John said and would have given all an opportunity to see the impact his remark had on the group's level of trust. In the course of this exercise John might have decided to name the person he had in mind. This information would then have been in the open where it could have been worked with. Looking back on it we could see the lesson that so often needs to be relearned: the damage done by what people say is rarely as bad as the consequences of what people keep themselves from saying.

"I'm afraid to look at what I'm really like inside."   As a symbolic way of exploring fear of Julie's inner conflict, we might begin by saying to her: "I'd like for you to stand by that closet door over there and pretend that some hidden dimensions of yourself are inside. Maybe you could open the door just a crack, peek inside, and report to the group as you do so about what you suspect may be inside." Or "Maybe you could stand inside the closet and, as you peer out at the rest of us, talk about some of what you fear may be in there with you that you are reluctant to let come out."

There's no telling in advance whether this exercise will become humorous or heavy. People can be insightful when in a playful mood, and Julie may quickly identify in a half-joking manner some of the fears she has about what might be locked up inside her. Or Julie or someone else in the group may have had a childhood experience with closets—being put in one as a punishment for the expression of feelings unacceptable to their parents, for example; such experiences can lend power to this exercise. In either case, by urging Julie to physically move in the room to undertake this suggested activity, we make her a tangible focus of group work and feedback, a real part of the group.

Other techniques could be used here. We might ask Julie to list all the fears she can spontaneously come up with. She could make this list by completing these sentences: "One thing I am afraid of is . . . . And this reminds me of another thing I am afraid of, which is . . . ." In this form of free association we are encouraging Julie to identify the specific objects of her fears. We can then ask her to develop a hierarchy of her fears, from things feared least to things feared most. After she has done so, we can teach Julie and the other members a relaxation exercise and then help Julie identify a pleasant situation and introduce a guided fantasy based on that situation. Each member can then describe a scene involving one of Julie's fearful situations, beginning with the least fearful. As soon as Julie experiences anxiety, she can signal by raising her thumb, and at this time the relaxation exercise and the pleasant fantasy are reinstituted. In this way, Julie can learn to face some of her fears and gradually be desensitized to them. This technique also brings in the rest of the group, and others may learn vicariously.

"I can't see why we have to share our feelings. What good does that do?"   James makes this remark after there has been much intensity in the group. The leader can begin by finding out whether anyone else in the group has the same doubts. Those who do can sit in the center of the room and talk to one another about why it is useless to express so much emotion. This technique gives these people an opportunity to express out loud some of the resistance they are experiencing; this resistance may otherwise inhibit the group's progress. This technique also gives these people, indirectly, an opportunity to do the very thing they are concerned about: to express some of what they are feeling. The leader might ask them afterward how they feel about having expressed these concerns and may thus encourage them to go even further. Another way to pursue this attitude is to ask these members to talk about what they may have experienced or have been taught about expressing feelings. Another technique is to set up a dialogue between members who are emotionally reticent and those who have shown some emotional intensity. After a few minutes, these people can exchange sides and try to put themselves in each others' places.

When a member like James voices a concern about expressing feelings, you should be aware of several possible dynamics. James's own way of recognizing his feelings may work well for him and yet be less dramatic than the way others in the group recognize their feelings. Or James may be expressing widespread group resistance; if so, this resistance needs to be explored. Or James may be afraid of his own feelings. In this case you might use one of the following techniques:

- "When in your life might you have learned that it is better to keep feelings to yourself?"
- "Would you be willing to state to each of the people here whom you have experienced as fairly emotional what you get from keeping the sorts of feelings they have expressed to yourself?"
- "If your parents were here, what would they say about all this expression of emotion?"
- "Go around to each person and speculate on what he or she would think of you if you expressed more emotion."
- "Would you talk about the worst things you could imagine happening if this group were to continue expressing so much feeling?"
- "Suppose you decided today to keep your feelings very much to yourself. How do you picture your life ten years from now if you stick to this decision?"

You may or may not want to go looking for relevant childhood lessons at this point, but when a client is fearful of the affect expressed in a group you usually can be sure that these lessons are relevant. Many people were taught as children to inhibit their emotions, while others witnessed devastating consequences of the expression of feeling. Any of the above exercises is likely to bring to the surface the early decisions James may have reached about the dangers of letting feelings be known.

"I'm confused and don't know what to do."   A statement such as this can sometimes be a form of resistance on an unconscious level. It may come from children of rigid and authoritarian parents. In some fashion the therapist is seen as a parent trying to get the client to do some work.

Of the many techniques for dealing with this resistance, here is one way the work might go. After Betty says she is confused, the leader says "What is it that you feel like doing now? What is the urge?" Betty replies "I want to pull back." The leader says: "Okay, pull back. Maybe go back behind the sofa and when you feel like saying anything say it." The leader then continues with whomever in the group wants to speak. After a while Betty rises to her knees and peers from over the back of the sofa. The leader asks "Is there something you would like to say?" Betty replies "No, I just want to stay here." The leader allows her to do so by stating "That's fine, but whenever you want to say something let us know." In a few minutes Betty breaks in and says "I want to come back in." Once she has done so, the leader says "Now that you are in is there anything you want to say or do?" Betty states that she would like to sit between Al and Pete and have them close to her. The leader continues "Now what would you like to do?" Betty replies "I would like to lean against Pete." The leader asks Betty what she would like to say to Pete. Betty says "I feel like a little child." "How old are you?" the leader asks. "Twelve." "What would you like to say to Pete now?" At this point Betty needs little assistance, and she is likely to talk about a painful childhood experience involving a parent.

When a client like Betty makes a statement such as "I'm confused," it should be clear to the leader that she is stuck and unable to proceed. Directly confronting her often just entrenches the resistance. In agreeing with Betty and in a sense handing the direction of the work over to her, the leader leaves her with no one to resist. All the leader needs to do is say: "What do you want to do now?" "What do you want to say now?" "Do whatever you want to do." This technique bypasses resistance by having the leader join the client in her resistance and allowing her to lead the way.

"I'm afraid to get close to people."   The leader can begin by asking Carolyn whether she wants to explore this issue. Does she really want to get close? Is it all right with her if she doesn't? Whom does she want to get close to in her life right now? Sometimes it is not clear how genuinely people are involved with issues they introduce. By asking Carolyn these questions, the leader can allow her to focus on whether this issue is pressing for her or whether she is getting what she wants as things are now.

If, as Carolyn talks, the leader comes to feel that although this is a significant topic for her, she is not expressing much feeling, he can ask her to talk about the closeness she feels is missing between her and others in the group. This technique brings the rest of the group into her work and provides an opportunity for feedback from others about whether she behaves in ways that keep her from having much intimacy with them. It also picks up on Carolyn's use of the word *afraid* and gives her an opportunity to discuss what the fears might be. These are some possible implications:

- She may have lost someone important to her either through death or the dissolution of a relationship.
- She may feel that there is something about her that people will not like if they get close enough to be aware of it.
- She may feel that intimacy with another will lead to her feeling smothered or trapped.
- She may be hurting over a divorce.
- She may fear too much commitment or too many demands.
- She may be uncomfortable with being accepted or loved.
- She may have had overprotective parents.

If Carolyn's fears of closeness stem from parental injunctions and tacit communications such as "Don't get close" or "Don't get committed," the leader can pursue the topic by asking questions such as these: What specifically did she hear from her parents or learn nonverbally? Who in her life told her not to be close? Next Carolyn can pretend she is that person and stand up and lecture the members on why they should not get close to anyone. What would this person—perhaps her mother—say about Carolyn's getting close to each member of this group? And what would Carolyn want to say in reply to her mother? Through this technique Carolyn can come to understand how she carries out these parental injunctions by being the way she has been in the group. The leader can continue by getting her to look at early decisions she made, such as "If I don't get close, I won't be rejected" or "I'm not going to be hurt again by being abandoned." The leader can then return to how she currently keeps herself from closeness in the group and in everyday life.

Carolyn thus can express her dissatisfaction with her lack of closeness and can learn that the roots of her difficulties with closeness lie in decisions she apparently made as a child. She then has an opportunity to consider whether to change the decisions that may have been appropriate for her as a child but that are no longer useful to her.

One way of wrapping up this work is to ask Carolyn to express to each member of the group a new decision she is considering about how much closeness she may want to seek with each of them.

"I can't identify with anyone here."   Sam, a retired executive, came to the group because of pressure from his wife, who complained of his being unfeeling. He rarely makes contributions in the group except to say what he thinks is wrong with others and how they ought to pull themselves together and be done with their problems. He usually looks critical and impatient. Finally, Patricia says she wishes he would open up more. He replies: "I can't really identify with anyone in here. Maybe it's the age difference between most of you and myself or maybe it's just that you people have different sorts of concerns from mine." Here, the leader can suggest exercises such as these:

- "Tell everyone in this group, Sam, how you are different from him or her and then add '. . . and I'm very different from you.' "
- "Go outside the group to enhance your sense of distance. Then talk to us about how you feel being outside."
- "Stand on a chair, above everyone, and tell us how you are different from each of us."
- "Say to each member of this group something you might have in common with him or her."
- "Pick the person you feel the most like, and tell that person how you are alike."
- "Now pick the member you identify with least, and tell that person how you are not alike."

This technique encourages Sam to check out his assumptions. His lack of identification with others may be a defense. He may explore the loneliness that results from being unable to identify with anyone, or he may get some insight into what he gains from being an outsider.

After this go-around, the leader can ask Sam whether he feels any differently and whether he is interested in exploring separateness from others as a possible theme in his life. She might ask him whether separateness characterizes his marriage. "Could you pick out the person here who most reminds you of your wife, and talk to her about what you have been saying to us? Perhaps you could say to her some things you haven't said before." Sam may say: "I can't do that. No one here reminds me of my wife. I don't see what good this would do."

In dealing with Sam's resistance the leader must be aware of how Sam is affecting her and ask herself how much investment she has in leading him further than he seems to want to go. She may need to remind herself that Sam has spent a lifetime not expressing himself. Here again, a good technique is to join him in the resistance: "Okay, Sam. No one here is going to make you do anything you don't want to do. You are going to have to tell me what you want." Or, if she has a hunch that he wants some prodding, she can push him a bit further: "Well, Sam, maybe nothing will come of this. But, if you are willing, I would like you to go ahead with speaking to someone here as if she were your wife. You might become more aware of feelings you haven't looked at if you try doing this."

Alternatively, the leader might try speculating out loud about what Sam may be thinking: "I've believed all my life that it's best to keep my feelings pretty much to myself. And as I sit here in this group I feel sort of like a visitor in a foreign country. I don't understand the conventions or language here." In using this technique the leader communicates to Sam that his resistance is respected. She shows that she appreciates how hard it is for him to open up and communicates to him and to the group that she is willing to respect his struggle and is available to hear him when he is ready to be heard. This technique is somewhat directive, but if it goes nowhere the leader can drop it. The leader's speculations may be wrong, but they may give Sam food for thought and they will give the rest of the group some sense of Sam's being included.

Working with a client like Sam can be one of the most difficult tasks a leader faces. Sam can easily become the target of group hostility, but that hostility will probably do nothing more than increase his defensiveness. If the leader is insecure about her abilities, she may use Sam as an excuse to forget her responsibility to the rest of the group and may blame herself for Sam's resistance.

"We seem stuck in our group, getting nowhere." In addition to looking at their own responsibility when members make such a statement, leaders need to explore the dynamics in the group itself that are slowing it down. This is not the time to introduce a technique to get things moving. A lot is happening in the group; the problem is that members are not expressing what they are thinking and feeling— on some level they are choosing to remain stuck. Using a gimmick to reduce the anxiety in the room takes the responsibility away from the members to go beyond the point of being stuck. A better technique is simply to challenge the members to say out loud some of the things they've been saying to themselves. This technique should bring into the open key issues that have been hidden and should provide an opportunity for a discussion and resolution of some of these issues. The leader may hear statements such as the following from the members; many of these concerns may not have been verbalized up to this point.

Sharon says: "I'm still not willing to say too much in here because every time I do people seem to jump on me. So I've decided to sit back and watch the game." The leader can begin by exploring with Sharon how she sees the group as a game. Then the leader can ask her to be specific and to indicate whom she perceives as attacking her. This approach might provide an opportunity for the leader to discuss with the group the difference between attacking and caring confrontation. Perhaps Sharon is defensive about even constructive confrontation. Or perhaps some of the members or the leader are being overly aggressive. This technique allows the leader to discover whether the block is within Sharon or whether this is a block for most members. If confrontation is generally being handled poorly by the group, then the leader needs to both model and teach a more effective way of confronting.

Janice states: "I'm afraid to really let myself get involved in this group because I don't want to cry. If I begin to cry, I just might open up so much hurt that I won't be able to close up the wounds. So I am keeping myself reserved." Here, if Janice is willing to take the risk, she can talk about her most terrible fantasy of what would happen if she were to cry. What might it be like for her to open up wounds that she thought were healed? By pursuing this fantasy, Janice can get a clear idea of whether she wants to continue holding herself back.

Grant announces: "For me this group is scary. I'm afraid to open up for fear that if I do, then I just might go crazy." The leader can invite Grant to explore what he imagines it would be like for him if he were to go crazy in the group. He might be afraid of his anger or of hurting someone or of being perceived as different or of losing control. This more specific fear can then be worked with. Or Grant can explore his original fear in depth by disclosing to the group what he imagines it would be like for him to actually go crazy. What would he be feeling? What would others think of him? How would he deal with what he opened up in the group when he leaves the session? Again, these leads are all good ones for the leader to follow up, assuming Grant is willing to do so.

These examples illustrate that indeed a lot is going on within the group. Members are stuck largely because of their unwillingness to disclose to the group some of the things they are telling themselves. The basic technique here consists of encouraging people to bring out into the open their thoughts and feelings about how they are experiencing the group. This technique provides plenty of material to work with, and the group no longer stays on a plateau.

"I don't feel safe in here."   Jill declares to the group that she sees others as able to openly share what they feel and as able to talk about themselves in ways that are not easy for her. She adds that she'd like to be able to let others know what she's like, but somehow she just doesn't feel safe doing so. She agrees to work on what is blocking her.

The leader can use a number of techniques to help Jill explore ways that the group could become a safer place for her. One direct approach is to simply say: "Jill, I wonder whether you can tell us what it's been like in here all these weeks for you? Would you be willing to tell us what you've been feeling about the climate in here? How has it been for you to feel that you've had to hold yourself back?" These questions give Jill an opportunity to disclose what she has been feeling as a member of the group without putting her on the spot to talk about other personal issues.

If Jill is willing to say what she has been experiencing as a member of the group, she will probably provide many leads for further work. Jill may acknowledge her fear of being judged by some of the members. When asked to select one of these members, Jill picks Peter. The leader can then say: "Jill, would you be willing to look at Peter and tell him all the things that you imagine he'd be saying to himself or to others if you were to let him know who you are? It would help if you could say everything that you can think of without rehearsing. Just list all the judgments you can imagine Peter making of you." This technique can provide the basis for a dialogue between Peter and Jill. The rationale is to give Jill an opportunity to state what she is silently ruminating about and to allow her to check out her assumptions. Jill may be thinking that Peter is highly critical of her, that he doesn't like her, and that he could not possibly be interested in her. Peter's actual thoughts, however, may be that he'd like to hear more from Jill and that he misses her participation in the group. Unless Jill checks out her assumption, she will continue to operate as though it were true.

After the leader works with Jill, he might ask others in the group whether they feel the way Jill is feeling. If one or more members do feel unsafe in the group, they, along with Jill, can form an inner circle and tell each other all the ways they perceive danger in the group and how it feels for them to be in the group. They can also talk about what they can do to make the group a safer place for them. Other members can then provide feedback and reactions.

An alternative strategy is for the leader to ask Jill to zero in on what appears to be an underlying irrational belief—that everyone is judging her and that she must gain everyone's approval—and to evaluate the validity of this belief. The leader can suggest that Jill give the group a lecture on the supreme importance of being alert to the judgments of others and on ways to gain universal approval. The leader can encourage Jill to say how horrible it would be if everyone were not to win this approval. After her lecture, the leader can ask her to explore questions such as these:

- "Who told you that it is absolutely essential that everyone approve of you? How does this assumption prevent you from being the person that you want to be?"

- "What price are you paying to gain the universal approval that you are seeking? Is it worth it?"
- "Is what others think of you more valid and important than what you think of yourself?"
- "How much sense does it make to hold beliefs about others that you do not check out?"

Another approach is to ask Jill to monitor her behavior during the week and to make notes of the times and situations in which she feels judged. Jill can also record what she does in such situations, what she feels, and what she tells herself. By making such notes, Jill may become aware of how her inner dialogue creates her feeling of being judged. Jill can bring her notes to the group and report on the patterns of her behavior that became apparent to her. She can also think about how she might behave differently in these situations and then set up role-playing situations in the session to practice specific alternative behavior.

For example, Jill reports that she experienced much anxiety when she took her car back to the shop that charged her $150 for a poorly done tune-up. Although Jill barely made it back to the auto shop with her faulty engine, she quickly became apologetic when talking to the mechanic and did not insist that he fix the car without further charges. Consequently, it cost her an additional $50, which she felt was unjustified. All the way home she told herself how quickly she backed down and how her desire to gain the mechanic's approval kept her from being as direct as she would have liked to be. In the group session, Jill can practice assertive behavior with the mechanic through role playing. Others can give her clear feedback on specific aspects of her behavior that contribute to her ineffective style in getting what she wants when she thinks she is right. The members can coach Jill in saying certain phrases or using a different posture or changing the tone of her voice. Along with this assertiveness training in the group, Jill can also be asked to evaluate her underlying beliefs and thoughts to determine how they keep her from being the direct person she says she would like to be.

This and the preceding example indicate that the issue of trust is not settled during the initial stage of the group. It may surface again and again in the group's history, often following periods of intense emotion. The usual signals are silence, lifelessness, or superficiality. Leaders should remain alert to clues that trust is, once again, an unexpressed concern within the group and seek means for giving it expression in order to move on to personal issues. Jill, for example, first had to deal with her lack of trust both in herself to express what she was thinking and feeling and in others in the group before she could openly discuss personal matters. By working on trust, she freed herself to report "failures" without being frozen by the fear that others would think badly of her.

"This isn't the real world."   Cheryl brings up an issue that she wants to work on in the group. She is having trouble in applying what she experiences in the group to her life at work and at home. Cheryl feels free to disclose what she is feeling in the group, for she feels supported in doing so. She can get angry with someone in the group, state what is provoking her, and work toward a resolution of differences. Yet Cheryl is afraid that if she were to say what she felt on her job she'd soon be fired. At home too Cheryl is hesitant to be open with members of her family. She is afraid that they would not listen to her and that they would be hurt by her disclosures. Cheryl's basic task is to learn what is appropriate disclosure and how to make such disclosures without making others defensive.

One technique to use here is for the leader to ask Cheryl to describe a situation she is experiencing particular difficulty in and to state what she'd like to change in the situation. Cheryl says that she doesn't like the way she responds to her coworkers in the office. She sees herself as extremely careful of what she says to them lest she hurt their feelings and offend them. She constantly censors what she is about to say and attempts to figure out what her coworkers want to hear. She would like to feel free to tell these people what's on her mind, uncensored. After sketching the situation, Cheryl can select several "coworkers" from the group, describe an incident in the office, and tell how she typically would be in this situation. Then, she can try to tell each of the coworkers in the group things she'd not normally say, and she can say aloud what she is thinking and telling herself as she is talking with each of them. This exercise should uncover how she stops herself from being more forthright. She may be seeking approval from a coworker. Or she may be suppressing her anger over the way she feels treated by that person. She may be intimidated by another's sarcasm and put-downs. Depending on where the energy seems to be with Cheryl, the leader can eventually have her focus on one of the coworkers and say more of what she typically censors out. She can at least be encouraged to tell this person how she is feeling in the person's presence. After the role playing, both the members and the leaders can provide feedback to Cheryl by telling her how they might feel if they were her coworker. How willing would they be to listen to Cheryl? How were they affected by her?

Through the role-playing exercise Cheryl can learn a lot about the impact she has on others. Perhaps she demands that others be self-disclosing or in some way meet her expectations. Or she may focus on how she'd like them to be different instead of focusing on how she could retain her integrity in spite of the fact that some people around her are not willing or ready to change the way she'd like them to. In short, she can learn how to confront others without increasing their defensiveness. The specific feedback after role playing is helpful to members such as Cheryl who may not be aware of how their style of disclosure puts others off.

The leader might want to point out to Cheryl and others in the group that what occurs in a group can be realistic. Members not only can be open and trusting in the group but also can take risks selectively with people on the outside. The key word is *selectively*, for Cheryl can be setting herself up for failure if she attempts to open up with everyone she knows. She needs to decide how important a given relationship is to her. Cheryl may well decide, for example, not to tell her boss everything that she thinks, for she may indeed put her job in jeopardy by doing so. It is therapeutic for her to say what she typically keeps bottled up inside of her in the supportive atmosphere of the group, but it may be unwise for her to do the same at work. However, she can still recognize within herself what she is feeling, and she does not have to repress those feelings even though she keeps them to herself.

"If I started crying, I'm afraid I'd never stop."   Jane has held herself back through much of the group's life. When the leader asks about her behavior she says she is afraid that if she were to start to cry she might never stop. In such a situation, the leader might begin by pointing out that he has never yet seen anyone in a group cry for more than, perhaps, 20 minutes; when people show their feelings, these feelings tend to be short lived, but when people do not permit themselves to cry they may spend a lifetime being sad. Having said this, the leader can ask Jane whether she wants to try letting go of her emotional control. If she agrees, the leader can have her sit in front of Sally, whose eyes are still moist from work she was involved in a few minutes before. Keeping eye contact with Sally, Jane can talk about some of the things she holds herself back from crying about. The emotion still evident in Sally's face may serve as a catalyst for evoking feeling in Jane.

Or the leader can ask Jane to tell Sally how she is affected by Sally's tears. Jane may get through her resistance to crying by talking to Sally about her reaction. During this exercise, the leader might suggest any or all of these sentences for Jane to complete as she continues her contact with Sally:

- "I wish you hadn't cried, Sally, because when you did I . . . ."
- "If I were to cry like that I would . . . ."

- "If I were to cry, I would cry about . . . . "
- "One reason I can't cry is . . . ."
- "Tears don't do any good because . . . ."
- "The people in my life who cried were . . . ."
- "The people in my life who didn't cry were . . . ."
- "No matter what you do, Sally, I'll never cry because . . . ."

The leader can take cues for further work from Jane's replies. Sally also should respond by saying what it was like for her as Jane talked directly to her. Finally, to connect others in the group to this work, they can express to either Jane or Sally how they were affected by the interaction.

Although it's preferable for leaders to allow clients to supply the material with which they want to work (as in the case of Betty and her confusion), sometimes leaders may want to fish for material that they are not positive exists. Suppose Jane is willing but stuck. She is sitting before Sally and seems to have no idea what to say. The leader can try a hunch: "Jane I wonder whether there has ever been a person in your life whom you needed to cry over yet didn't allow yourself to?" In fishing for material the leader formulates a broad question that almost anyone could find something in to pursue. The leader may suspect that in fact Jane still mourns the death of someone important to her and that her grief contributes to her depressive style. But mentioning death here is too specific and threatening. Instead the leader gives Jane an opportunity and leaves her enough room to pull back.

"I'm afraid I'll go crazy."   Dave expresses his fear that deep down inside he has the potential for going crazy. He apparently sees craziness almost as if it were tangible, a thing inside him, like a tumor, that resides there undiagnosed. Assuming Dave is a member of a group composed of relatively well-functioning people, the leader can get him to work with the paradoxical idea that people gain control in their emotional lives when they become willing to lose control, when they give up rigid fears about what they would be like if they did not constantly keep their emotions in check. In doing such work, however, Dave may become hypnotically fascinated with acting like a crazy person to a degree that concerns the leader. At this point it may be appropriate for the leader to say: "You know, Dave, I'm finding parts of the way you conduct yourself a bit too bizarre, and I am frankly concerned that you are going to immerse yourself in this so much that you will forget how to pull yourself back. In a way, I think craziness is a possibility for all of us, and it's a possibility I see you as working too hard to make real. So in spite of the fact that I am generally encouraging people here to be unrestrained in their expression of feeling, I'd like to encourage you to realize that you really could be crazy if you insist on it; it might be more productive for you to work on calming down a bit and developing some coolness and a sense of perspective." However, the occasions when a group leader needs to suggest such restraint are few, especially when members are screened prior to joining the group.

In more normal circumstances, the leader might start out by asking Dave a question: "I wonder where you got the idea that you might go crazy, and I wonder what that expression might mean to you?" Dave may say that there is a history of mental illness in his family. Or he may have been told that masturbating or expressing anger can make people crazy. Next, the group leader might invite Dave and other members who have expressed this concern to stage a demonstration of how they think they might behave if they were crazy. Instead of staging a demonstration, Dave may say "I think I would just sit here in a stupor and not interact with anyone." Another member may reply "It seems to me, Dave, that this is pretty much what you have been doing in this group." The point here is both to acknowledge Dave's concern and to provide a vehicle for confronting it.

Leaders should keep several points in mind in connection with this example. First, all counselors and group leaders should think through their own theoretical positions about mental illness regardless of whether they work with institutionalized people or relatively well-functioning inviduals. Our own perspective is that craziness is a form of conduct a client chooses rather than a hidden force within the client. Not all readers will share our theoretical convictions.

Second, leaders must explore their own fears of being or going crazy. Leaders who are frightened by their own potential for bizarre behavior can easily reinforce the fears of a client working on this problem and of the rest of the group.

Third, counselors have no business taking clients further than they are prepared to go with them. If leaders are ready to accept and work with a client who fears going crazy, that client and all the group members will gain. However, leaders won't be doing anyone a favor by pretending to accept emotions with which they do not feel at home. What is perhaps most frightening to an inexperienced leader conducting a group composed of presumably relatively well-functioning individuals is to find that someone's behavior is bizarre to a degree that the leader finds unsettling. We indicated above one technique to employ in this situation. The request for the individual to stop performing those behaviors that the leader feels are bizarre can be made in the group or privately. Telling people to stop is not automatically going to make them stop, but it is a way of maintaining an honest relationship with them and a way of maintaining contact with them. Eye contact is especially important because it is easier to withdraw or numb oneself without it. In summary, then, leaders who find themselves uncomfortable with how far out a client is getting can be honest with the client about their concerns, can demonstrate their readiness to be with the client, and can insist on the client's staying physically and emotionally with them.

Experienced leaders tend not to be afraid of clients' being or going crazy, and this trust in clients is an asset to the work clients are willing and able to do. Among the fears that typically haunt a group, the fear of being crazy is one of the biggest; here, as elsewhere, the leaders' biggest concern should be for those fears clients are afraid to express, and leaders can help to make the group a place where clients can express and examine those fears.

Fourth, when people have done something in the group that they regard as crazy, it is important for the leader to follow up by establishing contact between them and the group; otherwise they often are inclined to withdraw. On completion of their work, these people can seek out feedback from the rest of the group; more often than not, this feedback is reassuring. Withdrawal is often the result of embarrassment, and contact with the other group members can alleviate this embarrassment.

Working with challenges to leaders

"You leaders aren't sharing enough of yourselves."   This sort of remark is a healthy sign in a group because it indicates that members are perceiving an inequality: the leaders are different from all the others in the group in that they don't say much about themselves. At this point leaders can abdicate their role if they throw out some historical piece about themselves to placate the group. Rather, they might indicate that they are in the group not for their own therapy, as are the members, but to be leaders. They can, of course, share ongoing feelings and thoughts concerning members individually and as a group and can acknowledge being touched by personal issues. But generally they can take up these issues with their own therapists.

Leaders also do not have to apologize for their role. The group is getting to know them through the way they pay attention to members; leaders become transparent in many ways without talking about personal problems. In other words, leaders do a disservice to themselves if they have to prove that they too are human. At the same time, leaders do not have to give the impression that they have arrived and do not need to work on themselves; they can let members know that they are still struggling with issues in their own lives but that they do not think it appropriate to pursue these issues in groups they are leading.

Leaders might examine the motives of people who ask them to show more of themselves than they do. They often are the same people who become angry with leaders for taking up group time with personal problems. Or they may become condescending after leaders share an issue of their own, such as a feeling of inadequacy. Often such a challenge is based on the members' need to relieve their own anxiety, to have some of the pressure taken off, or to bring the leaders down and make them less frightening.

One technique to use here is to ask the people making the challenge to talk further about what kind of sharing they want, to be clear about their expectations. If the challenge comes from one person, leaders might check it out with others. Leaders can then assess how disclosing they have been, and, if they see things differently, they can dispute the members' challenge. If, however, the challenge does have some truth, leaders can admit it and perhaps attempt to give an explanation. If many people give essentially the same feedback, these people can form an inner circle, with the leaders in it, and deal further with their responses to the leaders and the leaders' responses to them, sticking with here-and-now responses only. This technique puts into the forefront the leader/member relationship and its effects and shows how this relationship can interfere with the members' doing as much work as they can.

Some leaders may feel comfortable sharing not only present reactions but old feelings that come to the surface because of someone else's work. This material can be a catalyst for further group work. Leaders should not display these issues and feelings, however, simply because group members want them to. These leaders may find that attuning themselves to their feelings, both those that arise in the present context and those nurtured through reminiscing about their past, does not detract from their ability to be fully attuned to other people and their work, but on the contrary, tuning into these feelings is their best tool for listening to others. They may want to spend some time before a group and during breaks reviewing and focusing on past and present concerns in their own lives.

Other leaders may be less interested in getting in touch with feelings in themselves as a prerequisite for leading. If the feelings are there or if they come up within the course of a group, they may express them, but they don't feel the need to stir them up. Some leaders also may not be able to switch in and out of their own intense feelings fast enough to keep their primary focus on the client, to be fully with the group member's work rather than their own. If a personal issue interferes with being with the client, leaders may work on it in the group but only in order to get clear enough to continue work with the client. It is important, however, for leaders to bring into the group any persistent feelings they have that stand in the way of their being able to work with a client. For example, if a leader reacts to a client with anger, boredom, or annoyance, the leader may not immediately share these reactions. However, if these reactions persist and get in the way of working with the client, the leader eventually will need to share these reactions so that they do not interfere with the leader's relationship with the client. If leaders are trying to teach members that feelings are all right, one of the best teaching aids they have is to express feelings themselves.

The main point here is that leaders should not be working on their own material in the group at the expense of the client. If a member brings up a fear of being inadequate, leaders can mention similar concerns of their own in a way that encourages the member to go further. But if the whole group stops so that leaders get to talk about their feelings of inadequacy, then the purpose of the group has been lost, and the role of the leader is blurred. If leaders are involved in their own growth, as they should be, they will find that most personal matters can be postponed for discussion with their own therapists.

"You leaders aren't doing your job right." This challenge can take many forms. Members may say that leaders ". . . don't really care for us," ". . . are against us," ". . . are directing us too much," ". . . aren't directing us enough," ". . . aren't getting us started," ". . . are pushing people too much," ". . . leave people hanging," ". . . focus too much on pain and hurt," ". . . are using this group to fulfill your own needs," ". . . don't really know what you are doing," ". . . seem to have a lot of hangups so how can you lead us?" One technique is to say: "Well, time's up for today. See you next week!"

More seriously, this challenge can be seen as a healthy signal that a group is becoming autonomous. In this situation, you cannot become defensive; you cannot simply dismiss such confrontations as a stage the group is going through, nor can you too readily assume that you are failing.

One technique for bypassing defensiveness is to share how you feel about what has been said and then to see whether the rest of the group shares the perception of the member making the challenge. At a moment like this you can model the kind of behavior you hope the group members will learn, including a willingness to explore matters that trigger off a defensive posture.

Another technique is to share with the group members how much validity you see in their statements, acknowledging parts that strike you as true and denying parts that don't seem to fit. Typically, there is some truth and some misperception or projection in such confrontations, and this technique helps sort out the truth. Parts that are true sometimes need to be explained. For example, one leader was told during a group session that he seemed to be sitting back and not working with people who introduced material they wanted to explore. The leader explained to the group that he had indeed been holding back because he felt that the group was doing so much advising and questioning of one another that the group's progress was being undermined. By sitting back and letting this process continue, he hoped the group members would eventually come to see what they were doing and decide to become working members again rather than advice givers.

Another technique is to ask group members how they would like things to be different, if indeed they would, and then to state whether you, as a leader, are willing to do what the members want and why. For example, members may say that they want you to introduce techniques when they feel stuck or when there are long silences; and you might reply that you do not want to take on too much responsibility, that the group shares the responsibility for what gets accomplished. This technique allows members to clarify what they want and allows you to discuss your own views openly. In fact, you might respond initially to a challenge by stating what you would like to see going on in the group.

In the techniques suggested so far you, as a leader, seek to acknowledge the true parts of the challenge. Of course, you can also explore the possibility of projections. Complaints are often more important for what they say about the members than what they say about the leaders. If you have modeled receptiveness and an ability for handling situations in which you feel defensive, you are in a good position to ask group members to explore the part of themselves that finds fault with others.

"We seem stuck in our group, getting nowhere." When group members collectively voice this complaint, leaders might reflect on their performance by asking members how they perceive the leaders' expectations of them as participants. Groups sometimes bog down when they sense that the leaders have expectations for them that differ from their own. The leaders may want more for and from the group members than they want for themselves. For example, the group may have collectively decided to settle for superficial interchanges, while the leaders are hoping that they will push themselves to a deeper level of communication.

Deadness in a group sometimes results from a change in style on the part of the leaders. At times leaders may prefer to stay on the side lines, observing and commenting on the interaction among members. At other times leaders may be constantly involved in the dialogue. At yet other times leaders may play a directive role in the group, promoting interaction among members. When leaders have been using either of the last two styles and then switch to the side lines for a while, the group may get stuck because members have learned to expect directive input. In such cases leaders must acknowledge their responsibility for the period of stagnation. If they change tactics without warning or if their own energies fail, the group simply may not be used to finding its own way. To avoid this possibility, leaders can simply say that for the next half hour they will stay on the side lines to give the group an opportunity to find its own direction. This statement can be made without defensiveness or hostility.

Leaders may also want to step to the side lines when a group seems stuck because the deadness may have been created originally by the leaders' directiveness. Leaders should also, of course, be alert to the opposite possibility—namely that they are providing too little structure.

"You guys blew it."   Every novice group leader worries about making mistakes. In one sense, any input you give as a group leader can provide material worth exploring. Regardless of whether group members think you are marvelous or a flop, the way they respond can teach them much about themselves. And, although you are still going to worry about being good and effective, you will function better once you begin to worry less because you then free up your spontaneity and intuition. For all that, all leaders have moments that qualify as mistakes—interventions they regretted, techniques they would have preferred to have used differently. Mistakes occur when leaders impose their own agenda rather than being sufficiently ready to follow and flow with the client.

The most economical and appropriate technique for handling a misdirected technique is to admit the mistake. We've rarely felt that we lost the respect of our clients when we admitted our mistakes but have found that troubles multiply if we are unwilling to admit mistakes and try to forge ahead. It's a perfect opportunity to model making such an admission without undue defensiveness or remorse. Usually the emotional momentum that may have been dissipated by the inappropriate intervention can be recovered after such an admission. Sometimes it can't, but the issue that was lost may come up again. The important points here are that you not hide behind your role or assume you must be perfect and that you not try to cover up a mistake by imposing yet another technique. As long as you are not trying to hide behind a bag of tricks, it may sometimes be productive to create a technique for constructively exploring your group's reaction once you've gone wrong.

Having discussed some general guidelines that you can use in dealing with mistakes you may make as a leader, we now provide a list of mistakes that we've sometimes made as group practitioners:

- We have given instructions that were too elaborate, complicated, or obscure.
- We have been too hasty in introducing a technique when we were not clear enough about what our clients were saying or not clear enough about where we wanted to go with them.
- We have not been sufficiently sensitive to a client's resistance to going along with a technique.
- We too rigidly have pursued an outcome we expected a technique to have and were not sufficiently tuned into where the client was leading us.
- Our interjection of humor or our introduction of a humorous technique has been out of tune with a client's seriousness.
- We have lost the momentum of work in progress by taking too much time setting up a technique or looking for props.
- We have artificially imposed a technique that worked well when it emerged spontaneously within a session in another group.
- We have timed techniques poorly, usually because we were not sensitive enough to the client's own pace and were too fixed on our own interpretations or hopes concerning the client.
- We have used the technique of leader self-disclosure inappropriately—when, for example, we were tired at the beginning of a group and thus were burdening the members with our disclosure.
- We have introduced feedback techniques that give too much too soon and thus overwhelm the client.
- We have set up role-playing situations in which we have asked people to take parts that we forgot would be painfully inappropriate for them.
- We have introduced techniques for generating material when we were insufficiently attuned to hidden agendas and issues already present in the group.
- We have had techniques and catalysts in mind for a session and have failed to realize we had too much planned or have failed to be sufficiently attuned to the issues and moods our members brought with them.

- We have introduced an icebreaker technique to get things going when there was no need for it; the group was already prepared to work.

Working with intense emotions in all members simultaneously

Many people in a group may simultaneously become involved in expressing strong emotions to the point where they may feel that "everybody here is going crazy." Such chaotic scenes can be, depending on the group, productive and positive experiences. They often occur in groups with an intense format, such as a marathon; they result from a buildup of emotion, over time, in several group members. There are procedures for attempting to induce this phenomenon, such as heavy breathing and neo-Reichian techniques for working with body posture. We generally prefer to allow such whole-room catharses to emerge in their own way without prompting. It is almost impossible to predict just what will trigger off such events. The alert leader can be sensitive to this development (coleaders are an asset here) by staying attuned not only to the person working but to others in the group. Often the leader does not even have to do this much. Someone who is experiencing a strong feeling occasioned by another person's work will simply intervene by blurting out what is going on with him or her.

How might you, as a group leader, work with several members who are at once caught up in their own sobbing and crying? One technique is simply to bring the focus back to just one person: "There seems to be a lot of strong emotion in this room. Maybe we could all try for now to stay with Charlie and what he's dealing with."

Or, if you sense that several members could benefit from a catharsis at the same time, you can invite them to sit in the center of the group facing one another and to share their feelings. Others may be added to this inner working circle either at their own initiative or with your prompting. You need to have sufficient trust in this process to allow it to take its own course and must not be so concerned with keeping the focus on the person who had been working as to short-circuit the emergence of this phenomenon. You may make a mental note to come back to the person who had been in the spotlight when there is an opportunity later.

Once many people have begun expressing their emotions, you have to make a quick decision about whom personally to work with. If there is much chaotic sobbing throughout the room, you may want to move near or next to that person. At the same time you must glance constantly about the room to keep track of what is going on elsewhere. At this point, all the participants are potential resources for one another and can work constructively with each other. You may, with a word or gesture, pair people together either to have those people explore what they are feeling with one another's assistance or to offer comfort and support to each other. In doing so, you can draw on recollections of which people have interacted in what ways and of who seems to symbolize what to whom. Such pairing up can produce moving results. The woman who has been type-cast as the group mother, who always tries to soothe another's pain and never expresses her own, may sob like a baby in someone else's arms; the man who has said he fears being incapable of loving may cry silently and joyfully as he lets himself be with and comfort another. Thus, you need to trust a hunch to pair up someone who seems to be holding back emotion with someone else who could receive support from that person, or with someone who could perhaps prompt that person into letting down his or her barriers. You also need to be aware of individuals who may do physical harm to themselves or others, and it is important that you be ready to enlist the help of other members in physically restraining these individuals.

For various reasons, you may decide that some members are showing an excessive degree of emotion. The procedures one would ordinarily use to intensify emotional expression can be reversed to help a person gain distance and perspective. For instance, one can intensify a member's work by asking him or her to talk directly to the person with whom he or she has an issue. To deintensify the expression of this member, you might say: "Your mother isn't really here right now. I'm here. I'd like for you to look at me and talk with me about the feelings you have just been expressing and about what you want to learn from this work."

These groupwide catharses don't go on forever. That is perhaps the most important thing for the inexperienced leader to realize. Eventually the group calms down. A glance around the room reveals a lot of moist eyes, a lot of comforting and tenderness, perhaps some laughter, and a few dazed or frightened people who have stayed on the side lines. As the room begins to come back to normal, you may suggest that the group return to the original seating arrangement. You can then check in with the person whose work triggered off the chaos and find out whether he or she is feeling unfinished or cut off. You can also encourage those who did and those who did not become swept up in the event to discuss what they were feeling while it was going on. It is important for you to solidify the lesson that should be apparent, that people can allow themselves a period of intense emotional release and be left sane, intact, peaceful, even joyful.

The material people express during such cathartic sessions can be important and profound, but it is easy for individuals to forget what they were thinking and feeling and saying soon afterward. Therefore, as soon as feasible, all members can recall aloud the specifics of what they were experiencing and can try to focus on the insights and feelings and phrases they want to remember and learn from.

Working with dreams

"I had a dream." Patty reports a portion of a dream that she would like to explore. Here are some ideas for working with her. She can report the dream in the present tense, as if it were taking place now. If she can't remember part of the dream, she can invent the missing part, "dream it up" right now. As she presents the dream, you can pay attention to her voice, her level of energy, her body posture, and the parts she seems to gloss over as unimportant. At the end of her report, she can state how she felt on awakening, how she felt during the dream, and how she felt while reporting her dream. She can state what she learned from the dream or how the dream might tie in with what is going on in her daily life. In short, you can try to get an initial sense of what she might think the dream means. To work on the dream in more detail, Patty can assign different parts of the dream (persons or things) to various members of the group and coach the members on what they might say in those roles. She can tell each person why she picked him or her for the part, why that member was well suited for it. Patty can also be each part of the dream herself and carry on a dialogue with the other parts. If she was walking toward a door in her dreams, she can be the door and talk to Patty and then be Patty and talk to the door. You can also try to utilize props available in the room. For instance, Patty can have a dialogue with an actual door. Patty can also construct a different ending for her dream. Then she or others in the group can act this new ending out.

Another technique for working on the dream in detail is to invent sentence completions from the key phrases or concepts in her dream. For example, Patty can start by saying "If I were a door I would . . . ." Or, if she used the word scared in reporting the dream, she can complete several versions of the sentence "What scares me most in my life right now is . . . ."

To involve other members more directly, those who seem especially interested can talk about the dream as if it were their own and can act out various parts. Or they can free-associate to what they regard as interesting symbols in Patty's dream. The group members can also argue over and decide which parts of the dream they want to act out according to their own fantasies. The point here is not for them to interpret for Patty but to use her dream as a tool for looking at themselves.

Techniques for working with dreams can be modified or abandoned as other issues or reactions from others in the group begin to surface. Involving other members allows you to use Patty's dream for working with Patty and others in the group simultaneously. Often also, simply allowing the client to report a dream without elaborate attempts at interpretation is valuable. There may be little necessity for the use of techniques at all.

"I had a dream about the group."   Often during a weeklong residential group a member dreams about the group. Melissa had such a dream on the second night: "I am in the back of a big tractor with Patrick [a leader] driving it. The tractor has no trailer attached, just the cab. We are driving through this small town when suddenly faceless people stop our cab and start beating on the windows. I cry out to Patrick 'Do something,' and he says 'Don't worry, there is no danger.' I look around and these faceless people seem to be all over the place, attacking people in the town. But then I notice that nobody seems to get hurt and no harm seems to have been done." Even though the meaning seems obvious, Melissa can profit from interpreting the dream in Gestalt fashion.

She can begin by speaking *as Melissa:* "I am Melissa. I am in this big tractor with Patrick driving. I feel very safe and happy in here with him driving. I am going to curl up in the sleeping compartment of this tractor and go to sleep." *As Patrick:* "I am Patrick. I know what I am doing. I know where to take this rig, and I feel good about what I am doing." *As the tractor:* "I am a great big tractor. I am strong. I am made of steel, and I command respect wherever I go. I haul heavy burdens for long periods of time, and I provide safety to those who ride in my cab." *As the faceless people:* "We are faceless people. We terrify others. They cringe and try to hide from us, and they think that we are going to beat them up and kill them." *As Melissa to Patrick:* "Do something. You are the driver. You are supposed to help me. I trusted you, and yet here you are doing nothing to protect us." *As Patrick to Melissa:* "Don't worry. Be patient. You will see that no harm comes to anybody. You are safe in here, even though it looks dangerous."

Melissa obviously is struggling with trust, both of Patrick and how he is conducting the group and of the group members. The next step is to have Melissa tell the "faceless people" in the group how she sees them as dangerous and attacking. She can also tell Patrick how he is not protecting her.

Working with projections and other problems of self-awareness

"I can't talk to my parents."   In response to Dee, we are likely to say: "Let's see whether we can learn more about why you feel this way. I'd like for you to pick out two people here who you can pretend are your parents. Don't worry about whether there is any real similarity; all you need is two pairs of eyes to look at and try to contact as you proceed. Now I would like for you to talk directly to your pretend parents, and, if you feel ready, try to tell them a bit of what you find it hard to talk to them about. Or, if you would rather, you might try to tell them what happens when you attempt to talk to them that leaves you feeling that it can't be done." Dee can start off with the sentence "Mom (Dad), it's hard to talk to you because . . . " or "When I try to talk with you I feel . . . ." By talking directly to her pretend parents, Dee mobilizes feelings that she may avoid by merely talking about her parents; this exercise thus provides practice in communicating in a direct and honest way. This technique may lead to exploring the content of what Dee won't talk about with her parents, or it may lead to clarifying the process of that communication and how it is inhibited. Thus it provides Dee with an opportunity both for practicing what she experiences as difficult and for gaining insight into the nature of the difficulty.

Our request that Dee not worry about any real similarity between her actual parents and the pretend parents forestalls Dee's saying that no one in the group is much like her parents. That may be true, but it doesn't provide much to work with; and it bypasses the opportunity for Dee to get some practice as well as some insight. The pretend parents may turn out to be good substitute parents, and the material they open up can be explored either by Dee or by the group members who are the pretend parents. Depending on context and hunches we may want to encourage the pretend parents to respond to Dee. Or it may be best for Dee to get things out in the open without interruption. But an emotionally productive and relevant scene may emerge from a dialogue between Dee and her pretend parents, especially if she does some coaching or role swapping. Even inappropriate input from one of the pretend parents may be turned to advantage. For instance, pretend Dad may do more talking than listening until Dee becomes frustrated enough to say that in real life her father's similar behavior is part of the problem.

"My father would not speak in English."   This example illustrates how leaders might work with a person's voice and how they might encourage a person to use his or her native language. Carlos has been given the feedback that he sounds abrasive. There is gentleness in his eyes and in the content of his remarks, but he has a way of using his voice that leaves people feeling under attack. He acknowledges the validity of this feedback and wants to explore the theme further.

The leader can begin by asking Carlos to give feedback to others in the group but to do this by singing—the tune doesn't matter—rather than by speaking. Carlos may be embarrassed but willing. Such a go-around may be enjoyable for its humor and touching in some of its specific contents. This exercise primarily allows Carlos to experiment with the range and modulation of his voice, and it also allows important content to emerge. Drawing on clues from earlier work, the leader can then ask Carlos to think how the voice of each of his parents sounded to him when he was a child and to give imitations of each while saying "I'm reluctant to be gentle because . . . ." The leader may have a hunch that in many ways Carlos is reluctant to be like his father, a kindly man much belittled by Carlos's mother. Sure enough, the imitation of his mother comes across as abrasive. When he starts to present an imitation of his father, Carlos remarks "My father would not speak in English."

People often display a significant amount of resistance when asked to work in their native language. Talking in English can distance these clients, while their own language may bring back many painful associations. Nevertheless, even though the leader does not speak or understand Carlos's native tongue, Spanish, Carlos is willing to proceed by playing the role of his father talking to his wife (Carlos's mother) about what his kindliness has cost him. As Carlos proceeds the leader can be attentive to clues of emotional intensity and urge Carlos to repeat phrases that seem to bring Carlos closer to his feelings: "Say that again, please." Eventually Carlos stops after some anger and some crying. By using this technique, the leader demonstrates a willingness to stay with Carlos's emotions even when the content is unknown. The leader can then ask Carlos to review, in English, what his work has taught him. He may state that he is afraid to sound like his father for fear that women will treat him as his father was treated by his mother. Carlos can then try a new voice and say something to each of the women in the group. Other members may comment on how he now seems gentle and yet powerful and attractive. Carlos is not likely to leave the group with a permanent new voice, but he can see the options he has for a different style, and he can acquire considerable insight into how others experience him and the reasons for his abrasiveness.

"I feel the burdens of the world."   Judy seems so tired, so weary. At an earlier session she was confronted by Jack for being so

quick to try to rescue him when he was discussing a conflict of his. Judy revealed then that during her childhood she often took on the role of the family arbitrator, always seeking to smooth over quarrels between her parents. Today, after completing some work with Jennifer involving a great deal of sadness, Judy looks exhausted; when she is asked what she is feeling, she says "I feel the burdens of the world."

One technique for exploring her feeling is to have her exaggerate it: "Judy, would you be willing to pick up that stack of telephone books and hold them while you talk to us about the burdens you feel. I would like for you to really allow yourself to feel their weight, as you talk, and allow them to symbolize how ladened you feel." A bioenergetic technique to accent this burden further is to ask Judy to stand with her knees slightly bent in order to add to the experience of stress.

As Judy lists various burdens she is aware of, the rest of the group can be connected to her work by having her stand before each member, one at a time, still holding the books, and complete the sentence "You burden me by . . . ." "Jennifer, you burden me by being so sad. I want you to be happy." "Jack, you burden me with your anger. I want everything to be peaceful." After completing this go-around, Judy can make another round, this time using the sentence "I burden myself by . . . ." "Jennifer, I burden myself by worrying so much about your being sad." "Jack, I burden myself by thinking I have to be responsible for solving your conflicts." This technique gives Judy some insight into how she is responsible for the way she takes on other people's burdens.

At one point, standing before Charlene, she says "Mother, I burdened myself by wanting you and Dad to get along better." Here the leader can drop the technique in progress and replace it with one designed to pursue the client's lead: "Judy, why don't you just stay there in front of Charlene and continue to talk with her as if she were your mother. Let's hear more of how you may have burdened yourself as a child."

Eventually the work may come back into the here-and-now ways Judy burdens herself currently. Because people are often reluctant to give up the things they complain of, the leader might now try a technique designed to facilitate looking at this phenomenon. Judy (who is still holding the telephone books) can continue on around the circle giving up a burden, and a book, to each group member. After she has completed this exercise and gotten rid of her books, the leader can ask her to make a contract: during the coming week if she finds herself taking on any of the burdens she just relinquished, she is to call one of the members of the group, whoever would be most appropriate, and ask to have her burden back.

The leader in this example draws on several modalities: Gestalt therapy, by asking Judy to exaggerate; bioenergetics, by having Judy bend her knees and experience her stress fully on a physical level; psychoanalysis, by asking Judy to experiment with incomplete sentences as a way to bypass resistance and gain insight; and behaviorism, by asking Judy to do homework assignments. The work in this example thus touches the three areas of thinking, feeling, and doing.

"Here, let me help you all."   Although not explicitly stated, Claude's underlying attitude seems to be "Let me help you all; I know how you feel; I was once there myself; I've got the answer for you." This attitude cuts off exploration. Although it is important for leaders not to ridicule a helping attitude, they need to distinguish between facilitative and nonfacilitative helpfulness. If Claude's nonfacilitative helpfulness is not dealt with, the group will slow down. It may be valuable to bring his attitude into focus by introducing a way of exploring it. For instance, the leader might say: "Claude, I notice that you seem ready to come to the assistance of people, and yet I get the impression that when you do so you seem to sap the energy from other people's work. Would you be willing to explore this?" If Claude agrees, the leader can suggest one of these go-arounds:

- "Go around to each person in the group and say "The way I could help you is . . . ."
- "Pick out some people here whom you would like to help with something they have shared and try to greatly exaggerate a helpful attitude toward them."
- "If there is somebody in your life who has been a helper, see whether you can become that person and go around to all members of the group and help them as that person would."

Why is Claude so anxious about letting others struggle on their own? Does Claude believe that the leader is not taking care of the group's needs and that he has to provide direction? These go-arounds give the leader a chance to discover Claude's motives. Perhaps Claude has believed all his life that no one will take care of him and that it is his duty to take care of everyone else. He may have been so burdened with taking responsibility for others that he does not see how he can behave any differently. To simply label him a band-aider is to ignore the dynamics his helpfulness may reveal. Eventually his work might be directed toward exploring ways he would like to be taken care of.

Why ask Claude to exaggerate being helpful when this is the behavior that seems to get in his way? By not trying to talk Claude out of how he feels, by giving him an opportunity to fully experience how he acts, the leader can get Claude to see clearly the implications of his behavior and to decide whether he wants to continue with his present style.

The leader could also use alternative strategies that involve cognitive restructuring in working with Claude.

• Ask Claude to list out loud all the reasons he has for helping others. Why is helping others so important? When did he make his decision that his place was to be so helpful?

• Ask the group to brainstorm on why Claude should be helpful and then ask Claude to evaluate each of these comments. Here Claude may begin to challenge his assumption that he should be helpful.

• Suggest to Claude that he ask for something in return from each person he attempts to help. Here Claude has an opportunity to experiment with a dimension of his behavior that is undeveloped; this approach calls to his attention his giving style.

• Have group members say to Claude each time he engages in helping behaviors "You're helping me again, Claude!" This technique makes use of other members to monitor Claude's behavior.

• Ask Claude to observe his behavior out of the group for a time and record instances where he puts his own needs in second place. Through this self-monitoring process, Claude may see ways in which he resists receiving from others.

We want to make it clear that we are not against a helping attitude, nor would we have an investment in getting Claude to adopt a me-first attitude. Rather the leader can use these techniques to help Claude discover for himself the one-sidedness of his interactions and how he affects others. His all-too-willing-to-help side can easily cause resentment in others, for they may feel continually indebted to Claude, while at the same time having little to offer him. After Claude gets a clear picture of how his behavior affects others, he can decide whether he wants to change this aspect of his personality. The group provides the context for Claude to see himself as others perceive him, and then he is equipped to decide what he will change.

"Nobody ever listens to me."   Julio says "Nobody ever listened to me when I was a kid, no one ever listened to me in school, no one ever listens to me at home, and I feel that no one listens to me here either." We might begin by asking Julio to pick out some members of the group who he feels are not listening to him and to explain what leads him to believe that they aren't. Suppose Julio gets feedback from the group that suggests he is right—people have found themselves not paying much attention to him when he speaks. We might then try in several ways to discover what it is about Julio that causes people not to listen to him.

• Ask the group members to give Julio specific feedback on the ways they perceive him as being difficult to listen to.
• Ask Julio to take on the personality of either of his parents and show how that parent might gain or lose the attention of the group members if that parent were in Julio's place.
• If one of the things about Julio that makes it easy to tune him out is his quietness, ask him to stand on a coffee table and loudly proclaim some statement that he wants people to hear.
• If Julio's voice is exceptionally flat and unmodulated, ask him to try to sing to the group about what he is feeling in order to find some different ways of being heard.
• Explore what Julio might gain from not being heard by asking him to work with a sentence starting "If you really heard what I was saying you would . . . ."
• Give him a homework assignment for the next week that will make explicit what we suspect are his underlying beliefs. Ask him to preface his remarks to people he talks to with "I know that what I am going to say isn't very worthwhile and you probably aren't going to listen to me, but . . . ."

It might be a mistake to stay too concretely with Julio's first remarks. We want to be ready to pick up clues as to what is really bothering Julio when he says he's not listened to. Maybe he has a history of feeling unloved, unimportant, unheard.

By using the techniques listed above, we are attempting to (1) get Julio to acknowledge his complaint and give him an opportunity to voice it, (2) get him to exaggerate those aspects of his behavior that might produce the situation of which he complains, (3) have others give feedback that will help Julio clarify what he might be doing or how others experience him, (4) have Julio discover where he might have learned to do what he does, (5) give Julio an opportunity to try out being different, and (6) give him feedback and, perhaps, positive rein- forcement for what he chooses to do differently. These techniques are not aimed at changing Julio. They provide a context for him to discover what he does, where he learned it, and how he could do things differ- ently.

This example illustrates how to combine exploring the here-and- now with examining the client's past. Although work may often turn out to emphasize family dynamics during the client's childhood, we typically start the work by looking at present feelings within the group. Then, if past history becomes relevant, the group members have already been made to feel included in the struggle, and they are ready to stay with the individual's work on past history and share the member's excitement as they watch for a transformation in present conduct.

"I'm confused and don't know what to do."   Betty's statement (in the section on fears and resistance) about being confused can be worked with in another way if we do not see it simply as an expression of resistance. We might begin by asking Betty to say more about what she is confused over. Often, confusion represents a pulling in different directions, and remaining confused prevents the person from taking a stand one way or the other. To accentuate these polarities and to provide Betty with a means of gathering more data so that she can clarify which direction she wants to take, we can include other members by asking them to take sides. For instance, if Betty has a dual urge to move close to people and also to pull back as soon as she begins to approach them, some members can join the get-close side and try to persuade her of the advantages of intimacy. Other members can take the opposite position and urge her to pull back, stressing the disadvantages of getting close to others. During this time Betty remains silent and allows herself to go toward each position. Then Betty can talk about what she experienced as she allowed herself to go back and forth. This technique is likely to touch other members who are struggling with similar choices, and these members can then talk to each other about their conflicts. In this way, the work of several members can be linked together.

"A part of me wants this and a part of me wants that."   Ambivalence, dichotomies, polarities—these are all extremely common in counseling work. Some common polarities are these: "Part of me wants to stay with my family but part of me wants to go back to work." "Part of me wants to push you away but part of me wants to have you hold me." "A part of me loves my Dad and a part of me hates him." "A part of me wants to live but a part of me wants to die." "Sometimes I feel important; sometimes I feel worthless." "A part of me trusts you and yet a part of me does not." "A part of me wants to feel; a part of me wants to go numb." Typically, we look for a means for each part to be expressed and try to assure the client that each part will have a turn to be heard. In this way, the client need not constantly cancel the force of one side by considering the other side simultaneously.

Polarities can have different meanings. If Fred voices a polarity, are both parts really parts of Fred, or does he want one thing and is introjecting the point of view of someone else who wants something different? If the two sides seem to genuinely represent him, then our objective might be to seek a means of integrating them and acknowledging both. If he clearly wants one side but feels he is supposed to want the other side, then our concern is to make this split clear and to present an opportunity to reject the foreign side.

One way to clarify the split is to accentuate it. A standard Gestalt technique is to ask Fred to sit in one chair while being one side and to sit in a different chair while being the other. This exercise has the advantage of bringing his whole body into play; movement symbolizes doing something rather than being stuck. And using two chairs allows us and Fred to clearly identify which side is being expressed; the moment Fred seems to be shifting to the other side in what he says, he should move to the other chair or be asked to do so.

We may look for clues about Fred's preference for one side or the other. Is his voice flat and dead in one chair, animated in the other? Is he comfortable in one chair, tense in the other? We want to be alert to the way Fred wants to go and follow his lead. Similarly, if he has introduced the dichotomy with "On the one hand . . . and on the other hand . . . ," we might ask him to let each of his hands represent a side. His clearly leaning to one side is a clue to his real preference.

In using a technique that accentuates polarities, the leader must be aware of when to request that Fred switch sides. The leader may not have to make the request; Fred may be aware of which side he is expressing and change chairs or hands accordingly. But he may need prompting to switch chairs if he unconsciously starts polluting one side with feelings from the other.

Polarities can also indicate that Fred is afraid to make a decision. In this case, however, Fred may prove to be much clearer about his choice than he wants to acknowledge. Sometimes all we have to say is "Pretend you do know which way to go" or "Take a guess" or "What don't you want to know?"

Another approach might be to ask Fred to consciously stay with just one side of his dilemma for the next week and to allow it to become dominant. Or we might ask Fred to assume that one side wins out and that he must stay with that decision for the rest of his life. How would that be?

The techniques mentioned so far do not include other group members in the work. We try to be constantly alert to the possibility of bringing in others who seem to be reacting or who have said something at another time that might connect with Fred's work. We also typically gear the exercises toward bringing in as many others as feasible, perhaps by using some of these techniques:

- Encourage others to share dichotomies of theirs that resemble Fred's.
- While Fred is speaking from one side, ask him to select someone else in the group to speak for the other side.
- Divide the group members according to which side of Fred's dilemma they feel closer to and have a group dialogue.
- Ask Fred to sit in the middle of the group and let others argue for the various sides.
- Have the group members vote on how they would prefer Fred to feel and then ask him to persuade them to change their votes.

In both this illustration with Fred and the prior one with Betty, the possibilities for involving other participants in one person's work become evident. Our bias is toward involving as many members as possible in an interaction rather than having the leader work with one person for a sustained time while the other members simply look on.

"I so much want your approval." Often people keep their thoughts to themselves out of fear that if they express themselves they will not have universal approval. They struggle with this issue in their everyday lives; and, within a group, if there is a norm about being disclosing, the pressure to take part conflicts strongly with their desire to withhold.

Herman asks for the leader's approval continually but indirectly. One technique here is for the leader to suggest that Herman tell her outright how desperately he wants her approval and that he write her every day of the next week discussing how much he wants this approval and describing all the things he has done that day that he hoped she would approve of. The rationale for using this technique is that by openly acknowledging what his behavior expresses Herman may be able to see clearly what he is doing. The exercise may soon come to strike him as funny, and he eventually may say "Hey, Mom, am I doing okay?" Even if this exercise doesn't eliminate his need for approval, it allows him to control that need. By laughing at his own behavior, he can come to understand how much his style is likely to annoy people.

Another technique is to ask Herman "Is there anybody in the group from whom you particularly sense disapproval?" If he thinks no one in the group disapproves of him, he can take on the role of each member of the group, pretend that person disapproves, and say what sorts of disapproving thoughts he supposes that person may have. The rationale for this technique is to uncover Herman's projections. If Herman picks out someone in the group from whom he senses disapproval, the leader can ask Herman whom this person reminds him of and then have him speak to the imagined person.

Herman can then pretend that he is that disapproving member and, as such, can say something disapproving to each of the other members of the group. The rationale here is that along with Herman's fear of being disapproved of there might be a strong desire to be critical of others; he may find that his real fear is that others will be as critical as he is. Often those who need approval excessively are also in many ways critical. An expected outcome is that this technique will both open up the group and bring Herman's own repressed criticalness or hostility into the open.

When a client is trying out a different side to his or her personality—for example, acknowledging a disapproving side—it helps to connect this work with a different posture. While Herman is speaking critically to others in the group, he is sitting on the floor with his arms hugging his knees. The leader might say "Herman, as you continue with this exercise, I'd like for you to stand up straight and point to each person as you say something disapproving to him or her." One outcome may be that Herman discovers that his suppressed criticalness can be constructive and that, besides, he becomes a more physically attractive person when he lets this side of him show.

"I'm empty inside."   Adeline says she is afraid to work any more: "My greatest fear is that if I *do* look at myself, I'll find that I'm empty and am simply a reflection of what everyone else expects. Now, at least, I can kid myself by saying that maybe I'm not so bad after all; yet if I *really* looked I just might find nothing inside. Maybe I don't have anything to offer anyone." In this case, Adeline may really feel empty inside or fear that she is empty inside, but she may also be holding back material she is afraid to acknowledge to herself or the group. In developing a technique for working with Adeline, the leader needs to be prepared to pursue either direction.

A common mistake of beginning group leaders in a case such as this is to try to talk Adeline out of what she says she is feeling, to assure her that she does have a great deal going on inside her. Instead, the leader might encourage her to experience even more fully what she feels.

Another common mistake is for the leader to assume too quickly that he knows what Adeline's words mean, rather than allowing her to say what being empty means to her. The leader can ask Adeline to select a visual image that symbolizes being empty. Suppose she picks a dead tree stump that is hollow inside. The leader can then direct her to become the hollow stump. She may say: "I'm dead and useless. I am rotten and decaying inside, of no use or value. There is no life left in me, nothing but dead and useless wood." Now the leader can try to have Adeline move from symbolic to concrete language taking his clues from words she uses that seem to invoke the most feeling in her and from whatever he happens to know already about her: "You mentioned being useless. Would you talk more about ways in which you are feeling useless in your life?" Or "You describe yourself as rotten inside. I wonder what's so rotten in there." These promptings may be sufficient to involve her on a feeling level in pursuing these themes. If she does not yet get close to much feeling, the leader can ask her to tell other members in the group something about her that is rotten or decaying or dead or empty.

Or if the leader suspects that what Adeline is saying connects significantly with the concerns of another member of the group, he can ask Adeline to talk to this member about her emptiness. Another possibility is to ask Adeline to talk to a member of the group whom she experiences as being full of life. By doing this exercise, she may discover that she hides behind her sense of deadness because she is jealous of those who seem more alive.

Although people who say they have nothing to offer others often may lack confidence, there is a hidden arrogance in their remark; they may feel that others have nothing to offer them. To explore this possibility with Adeline, the leader might ask her to tell group members something about them that she suspects is dead or hollow or rotten.

During the course of these exercises, Adeline may reveal that her sense of emptiness comes from the fact that she has devoted years to raising a family. Now that her children have lives of their own, she no longer feels she has anything to offer; in contrast she experiences others in the group as still young and vital and moving forward in their lives. Thus, the techniques will have brought material into the open in a way that promotes spontaneous interaction among the members of the group.

As an extension of her work, Adeline might take home a piece of dead wood as a reminder of what she explored and be asked to write each day for half an hour about all the ways she feels empty. She can bring her journal to the next meeting of the group and tell the members how it felt to allow herself to be empty and dead for part of each day. The rationale again is to give her an opportunity to experience her sense of emptiness fully.

Another way of working with Adeline is through the use of a guided fantasy. The advantage of this technique is that it includes the entire group. These might be the instructions: "I'd like to explore this feeling with you by starting out with a guided fantasy. The rest of you in the group might try going along with this to see what it brings up for you. Imagine some scene that represents emptiness to you. It might be a barren landscape or a dark empty house or whatever you like. Now I want to ask you to imagine entering into this empty place; try to be there. Let yourself feel the emptiness of the place you have entered: as you do so, tell yourself that what you are really doing is entering yourself and that you find that there is nothing there. Now I'd like for you to talk about what you notice as missing. For example, if you find yourself thinking that there is no capacity for feeling or for loving within this empty place, talk about that. I'd like to know more about what you call your emptiness."

Depending on where this fantasy goes, the leader can then perhaps try this exercise: "Now I would like to ask you to look around the room at the others, and when you see someone who you think has some quality that you find yourself empty of, tell that person about it; if you would like to take some of that quality from that person to fill your emptiness, tell how you could do so." This technique gives Adeline an opportunity to be specific about what she means by being empty inside and also promotes working with others in the group.

In this example, the techniques are designed primarily to provide Adeline with an opportunity to experience as fully as possible her emptiness as well as to acquire some insight into what she does that contributes to her feeling of being empty. If the leader believes that action on Adeline's part is also essential if she expects to change, he can challenge her to think of concrete steps she can begin to take to deal with her emptiness in a constructive way. Eventually Adeline may devise a plan involving new behavior designed to bring some meaning to her life. For example, she may decide to do some things that she has been saying she wants to do but has never found the time to do. She may thus come to recognize the range of options open to her with respect to behaving differently.

"People just don't appreciate me."   Bonnie wants to work on her feeling that people do not recognize her or appreciate her. She states: "No matter what I do or how hard I try, I still feel unappreciated. My kids are demanding, and I feel they just use me; and my husband rarely gives me support or tells me that I mean anything to him. He is demanding too, and I'm left feeling that I'm never enough. Even in this group I often feel unrecognized; I feel that I don't count and that what I do in here—or what I am—is not appreciated."

We might ask Bonnie to identify and talk to those members of the group (including the leaders) by whom she feels least appreciated. While she is doing this exercise, we pay attention to her style. Is she especially timid or affectless? Is there anything else about her that invites people not to take her seriously? We also want to find out specifically what she means by appreciation and get information about what she may want. We might give her an opportunity to list all the things that she does not feel appreciated for.

If we suspect from what she says that her feeling of not being appreciated has been with her from childhood, we might ask her to relive a scene with her parents when she felt unappreciated. She can be herself as a child and talk to her mother and father, using substitutes selected from the group, about what she is feeling: "Go back to that time, be that child, and, as if your parents were here now, say some of the things that you might have wanted to say to them." Bonnie may say: "You don't acknowledge what I do. Nothing I do seems good enough for you."

Then we might ask Bonnie to become either of her parents, with someone else in the group playing the part of Bonnie. Bonnie, as one of her parents, can talk about how nothing Bonnie does is good enough. Bonnie can imitate her parent's style of talking with her and attempt to express some of the things she fantasizes that parent may have left unsaid. By having Bonnie's substitute enter into this dialogue, we can involve another person in Bonnie's work and also give Bonnie an opportunity to see how she comes across. The substitute may also give Bonnie some ideas for an alternative and potentially more forceful style. This technique encourages Bonnie to verbalize some of the feelings she had as a child and then perhaps to discover how she may presently encourage people to treat her in the way she felt treated then.

These techniques can be followed with various cognitive approaches aimed at challenging the beliefs that influence Bonnie's behavior. In a number of ways Bonnie can be urged to critically evaluate her assumption that, regardless of what she accomplishes, it will never be enough. Some directions for further work can be found in these open-ended questions:

- "What will you have to do to feel that you *are* enough? What person are you seeking this external confirmation from, and, even if you attain this validation, will you *yet* be enough?"

- "How are you contributing to your feelings of inadequacy by clinging to the assumption that others *must* appreciate you?"
- "How valid is your conviction that you don't count unless others appreciate you?"

In general, the goal is to provide a context for Bonnie to think critically about how her assumptions and beliefs determine how she feels. She is likely to feel and behave differently if she successfully challenges some of her self-defeating beliefs.

"I don't like being overweight."   Frances is concerned about being overweight, but at the same time she says she likes who she is and is angry that people consider her heavy: "Fifty pounds overweight isn't all that bad." The leader may ask Frances to pick up some chains that approximate the weight Frances has described as excess. Frances takes the chains and continues to talk about whether she ought to try losing weight, interrupting herself occasionally to remark on how heavy the chains are: "Gosh, these chains are heavy. Why should I carry these things around? How much longer am I supposed to hold on to these? They feel so cumbersome. It hurts! I feel ridiculous holding onto these chains." When asked to stand before another member to tell him how it is to hold the chains, she says: "I can't. I can't move over there easily enough. I'm too inhibited by these things. And I wouldn't be able to get close to him."

Eventually, Frances may pause and reflect on the symbolic significance of the exercise and of her words. The leader can then ask Frances to repeat some of what she has said, replacing references to the chains with references to her own body weight. By speaking symbolically and then concretely, Frances may be able to reveal the limitations she feels herself to have as a result of her weight. When Frances finally drops the chains, she may remark: "I feel so light and free. I never knew how heavy 50 pounds could be. I have become so used to them I had no idea how much of a strain they are." The group may comment on the way she held onto the chains even though the leader had not instructed her to continue holding them. She could have gracefully declared her preference for putting them down much earlier.

At the end of the session Frances may declare her intention to go to a gym, which she was previously embarrassed to do. The leader can ask her to do a homework assignment when in the gym: occasionally pick up 50 pounds and reflect on what she has learned during her work in the group.

In this example, the resistance Frances probably would have felt to acknowledging that her extra weight was cumbersome and prevented her from getting close to people was bypassed by being approached symbolically. No one pushed her into losing weight: she had an opportunity to acknowledge her own dissatisfaction with those 50 pounds.

This example shows how props can be used productively to intensify work. We list here some other possibilities for using props to sharpen a point:

- Ask a member to stand inside an empty refrigerator box and peer out of a small hole while he talks to the group about how he feels boxed in.
- Ask a member to hide behind a blanket as she talks about her desire to hide.
- Surround a member with cushions and pillows to emphasize his fear of getting close and his desire for distance.
- Have a member express his feelings about his penis while holding a banana or a pencil stub.
- Have a member who feels she has not time for anything hold a clock or an egg timer.
- Ask participants to collect items that have some personal meaning for them: a rock, a branch, a leaf, an empty beer can, a book, a key, some fruit, a cigarette.
- Have a member hold a small pillow and talk to it as a small child.
- Have a member use a stack of cushions to represent people who are the targets of her anger.
- Have a member use an art object to stimulate fantasy.

All props, of course, should be used to intensify a member's work and not simply for entertainment purposes.

"We seem stuck in our group, going nowhere." In the section on fears and resistance, we discussed some responses group members might make when challenged to be specific about how they feel stuck. In addition to revealing their fears, their responses may indicate a lack of self-awareness or a lack of information about group process.

Ann responds to the question about being stuck as follows: "I don't seem to know what I want from this group. I have a hard time really deciding what I want to talk about when I come here. Things seem to be going pretty well in my life, and right now I'm not aware of any pressing problems I need to bring up." She may be stuck because she no longer wants to continue with the group. She may not feel a need to explore problems, or she may not yet be able to identify specific areas of her life that she'd like to change. Both these issues can be fruitfully pursued in the group, and as a result Ann might at least make the decision to withdraw.

Don says: "Frankly, I feel that we're not getting anywhere as a group because we never stick with a person long enough to solve that person's problem. What good does it do to just talk? If we're not providing solutions for problems we bring up, what good is the group?" In this case, the leader can deal with Don's expectation that a group is a place to solve problems; he may be expecting simple solutions to complex problems. The leader needs to assert that a group's purpose is not to solve problems but to give members a chance to identify personal issues and to explore various facets of these issues. Too narrow a focus on problem solving can encourage members to give advice and patch people up; such an orientation discourages people from expressing feelings.

Mary says: "So what should I do about my problem? I just don't know whether I should file for divorce or settle for the way things are in my marriage. I don't seem able to make this decision for myself, and I'm looking to the group to give me advice." Mary may be feeling stuck because she doesn't see herself any closer to a decision than when she entered the group. Here is a good opportunity to work with Mary's expectations of members and the leader. She may be hoping for an answer outside herself because she is unwilling to commit herself to a decision and accept the consequences of it or because she does not trust herself enough to make decisions. One way of getting her through her impasse is to have her look at the degree to which she is willing to take personal responsibility for her life. She may be using the group to justify whatever action she does take or she may be asking the group to make the decision for her so that she will not be accountable. These issues must be explored before Mary can hope to resolve her dilemma.

"Why do we always have to focus on the negative?"   Roz brings up the issue of her impatience with the leaders, whom she sees as expecting the members to continually come up with problems to work on. Roz continues by saying: "It seems that most of what we do in this group is focus on the negative. We always have to have some problem to talk about: there is so much focus on pain in here. I don't see what stops us from talking about some positive things. I get sort of depressed every time I leave this group because we are so preoccupied with digging into problems."

Before deciding on a technique to use here, the leaders can attempt to discover what Roz means when she states that there is too much focus on the negative. Here are some possible meanings:

• Roz may have learned to deal with conflict by avoiding it. When conflict surfaces in the group, she gets uncomfortable and attempts to do what she typically does in everyday life—avoid issues or attempt to smooth things over.

• Roz may have a lot of pain inside her that she is afraid to acknowledge. Having other members talk about their pain triggers her own anxiety, so she'd rather they focus on pleasant topics.

• Perhaps Roz is afraid of her depression. She may fear that if she allows herself to feel depressed, she will sink so deeply into a pit she won't be able to pull herself out. Thus, Roz would rather talk of positive things that won't lead to depression.

• Roz may be afraid of anger. For example, she may have experienced considerable anxiety when another member directed anger at her. Or perhaps simply observing others being angry scares her.

All these possible meanings involve fears and resistance. Techniques for working with them are given in the first section of this chapter.

If, however, Roz exhibited much feeling when she said that leaders expect members to continually come up with problems, the leaders might introduce a technique for working with her projections. One technique is to ask Roz to become one of the leaders. In this assumed position, she can talk to the entire group and tell them how they should act and what they should be in the group.

Once Roz's projections and expectations are out in the open, she can work on some of them. For example, one of the leaders might say to Roz: "In some ways you seem to see us as responsible for the negative feelings in the group, for after all we are the ones who are focusing on these feelings. We could direct the group in a different direction and avoid this focus. Do you want to go further with some of the directions you'd rather see this group take and what you'd want us to do differently?" If Roz answers affirmatively, she can say what she fears about each person and how she'd rather that person would be so that she would feel comfortable. She might tell Barbara to cheer up and count her blessings instead of dwelling on her misery. She might tell Bob not to get angry because his anger scares her. Again, the leaders can be listening for clues of where to go next with Roz. She may attempt to smooth things over in the group and focus on pleasant matters because she had the role of peacemaker in her family. If Roz would like to change her behavior in this regard, the leaders can then introduce techniques that encourage her to do so.

An alternative strategy for working with Roz is to ask her to complete sentences such as the following:

- "If the group continues this way, I will . . . ."
- "When people in my life express negative thoughts or feelings, I . . . ."
- "If only the leaders would . . . ."
- "This reminds me of . . . ."

This sentence-completion technique is designed to expose her reinforcement history and what she has learned throughout her life about negative experiences. The technique can generate material and provide data for further exploration.

"You guys blew it."   After Marilyn accuses the leaders of making a mistake and they have acknowledged their own responsibility, they can encourage her to talk about important people in her life who have disappointed her: "Talk to me as who I really am or as anyone you would care to address and tell me how you feel about my mistake."

If the leaders sense disappointment not only from Marilyn but from other members of the group, they can suggest that other members, as well as Marilyn, express whatever they may be feeling about the leaders. Again, leaders can't assume they know what the group is thinking, or why. The leaders' error may, for example, awaken feelings about other authority figures such as parents. In this case, group members might be invited to speak to leaders as though the leaders were parents.

"What I got out of that."   People often quickly forget some of the most significant insights or lessons that emerge in work they do in a group. Some therapists believe that people remember what they are ready to remember, but we disagree. We think that even though catharsis and insight are not followed by a lasting decision to change, clients can profit by thinking through—if only on an intellectual level—what they want to be able to recall subsequently. Tim's emotions are now subsiding, but he has just been through 20 minutes of work on several themes. He began by discussing a conflict he had been having with another member; in the feedback exercise that followed, other members praised Tim for several of his traits but criticized him for his sarcasm. This feedback led to role playing in which Tim imitated some of the sarcasm he recalled his mother directing at his father. Tim then began sobbing over the death of his father, and this work triggered off grieving in several members of the group. Now, as things are calming down, we ask Tim what he wants to learn from this work. Somewhat to our disappointment he replies "What I got out of that is that I am as sarcastic as my mother was and people don't like me for it." We had hoped he would remember more than just negative feedback, although remem-

bering only negative generalities is a frequent outcome of work in groups. What to do? Here are some possible techniques we could introduce at this point:

- Ask Tim to review each phase of the work he has just done and state succinctly the specifics that occurred.
- Invite as many in the group as care to do so to tell Tim what they most hope Tim will remember.
- Ask Tim to take on the role of each person who gave him feedback and repeat, as best he can, what that person said.
- Ask every person in the group who is willing to do so to write in Tim's journal something that he or she wants Tim to remember.
- Ask Tim to describe how he might discount what he got from his work.
- Ask Tim to go around the group explaining to each person who gave him feedback how he might discount that feedback. (For example, Tim might say he thought June was merely flattering him when she said she found him attractive.)
- Give Tim the homework assignment of writing about what happened in his journal.
- Ask Tim to look around the room and impress on his memory the faces of the members of the group as they look right now after having just been so intensely involved in his work. Ask him to try to recall the way these people look right now when, in weeks to come, he thinks back on today's work.
- Ask Tim to pretend that his mother and his father are in the room and to role-play each of them in summarizing what had been said.
- Ask Tim to state three or four specific lessons he wants to remember from what he has just experienced and to stand up as he declares these lessons to the group.

In the next chapter we discuss techniques for consolidating lessons learned from a group session and for remembering lessons learned over the whole life of a group. The point we want to emphasize here is that the process of reviewing and consolidating insights and formulating decisions about what to put into practice in daily life should be continually encouraged. The completion of a highly emotional segment of a session is a particularly appropriate time to create and introduce techniques highlighting lessons to be learned.

Concluding comments

In this chapter we have addressed the common themes that a group typically explores during the working stage. Our aim is to create and use techniques to facilitate the exploration of material that members give us rather than to use techniques to stir up material. We think it is important to take our clues from our clients and then devise techniques that will help them understand how they are thinking, feeling, and behaving. As can be seen in this chapter, we tend to avoid using pre-planned exercises or structured exercises as catalysts. We hope that we have made the point that techniques are most powerful when they are fitted to a given situation in a group as well as to the personality and therapeutic style of the leader. There is no "right" way to proceed with the material members produce. Instead there are many ways of creatively working with members to help them gain self-awareness and to provide them with the inspiration and encouragement to make changes they most want to make. We believe it is essential that you think about the rationale for the techniques you use and that you be able to discuss what you hope to accomplish by using them. Finally, at all times techniques must be used with respect and concern for the client. They are merely tools to facilitate self-understanding, not ends in themselves.

QUESTIONS AND ACTIVITIES

1. Review our account of the characteristics of the working stage of a group. Think about a group that you have led or in which you have been a member and describe how it did or did not attain this stage. Think about a group you have been in that did not reach the working stage and evaluate why, in your view, it did not do so.
2. In our discussion of Laura's concern about being liked, we explore the incongruity between her wanting to be liked and her clues that she looked at others disapprovingly. In the example, the leader tried to find a way to uncover her underlying feelings. Describe a technique that might be aimed at getting Laura to challenge her apparent belief that everyone must like her. Describe a different technique designed to explore the possibility that Laura's concern about being liked is connected with her childhood experiences.
3. A member of your group says "There is someone here I don't like." How would you handle this remark? What might you say? Would the stage of the group influence you?
4. Dee says that she can't talk to her parents. Develop several different hunches about what might be involved in this issue for her and explain different ways you might want to work with her.
5. Someone says "I'm afraid to look at what I'm really like inside." You suggest that she stand inside a closet and talk to the group about what she is feeling. The client declares an unwillingness to

follow your suggestion and is clearly anxious about the idea. What might you do now?

6. In asking Carlos to speak in his native language, the leader assumed that his feelings would be intensified by speaking as he might have spoken when the issues he was working on were more pressing. Explain some of your views about the possible connection between how one talks and the intensity of feeling, and describe some techniques that you think might amplify this connection. What advantages, if any, do you see to asking a person like Carlos to speak in his native language? How might you make use of others in the group who share Carlos's native language? How might you bring into this work others in the room who do not speak that language?

7. After reviewing our suggestions for working with Judy's remark that she feels the burdens of the world, review a discussion of the dynamics of depression in a textbook on abnormal psychology and develop some alternative techniques for working with Judy's statement.

8. Imagine a specific population you might work with, and suppose that a member of such a group were to ask you: "Why do we have to share our feelings? What good does that do?" What would you say? How would your response depend on the population?

9. In discussing Claude's wanting to be helpful, we propose that his attitude might have an inhibiting effect on others in the group. Develop a technique designed to explore how others in the group are affected by Claude's style. If you were to ask Claude to exaggerate being helpful, what would your theoretical rationale be? What might be the effect of asking Claude to do an exercise in which he avoids being helpful?

10. People have different ways of expressing their feelings and thoughts, and their styles may work well for them. However, they may be subjected to group pressure to express themselves in other ways. What are your thoughts on this pressure, and what are some responses you might make if you were to observe group pressure to conform to a norm?

11. In the example of Julio, who feels no one listens to him, we talk about the relevance of past history. If you are using this book as part of a class, have the class divide for a debate on the pros and cons of working on past material in a group. Do you think that a behavioristic viewpoint excludes considering an individual's past? What about a Gestalt or an existential point of view?

12. Betty says she is confused. In the example, the leader uses a technique for joining Betty in her resistance. If you used this technique,

how would you explain to a colleague or fellow student your rationale? Invent some techniques for directly confronting the resistance, and compare these with the approach we suggest.

13. Do some reading on Carl Jung and on Fritz Perls. How would you incorporate what they say about polarities into techniques you might invent for working with Fred and his ambivalence?

14. Suppose a member of your group says that you are not sharing enough of yourself. How would you handle this remark? What factors would you take into consideration? To what extent do you see your style as self-disclosing or as stating your own feelings or experiences?

15. In discussing Adeline's feeling of being empty inside, we suggest a guided-fantasy exercise. Write a guided fantasy you might use, and explain what you would expect to accomplish with the imagery you employ.

16. Develop a homework assignment for Adeline designed to have her explore her sense of emptiness in everyday life. Develop a different homework assignment designed to help her challenge irrational beliefs she may have about her emptiness.

17. Bonnie says people don't appreciate her. Describe a context in which you might ask the group to sing to her *My Bonnie Lies over the Ocean.* When and why might you ask Bonnie to sing this song? What might you hope to accomplish, and how might the result you hope for come about? When might you ask her to make up her own song about people not appreciating her, and why might you ask her to do so?

18. Adlerians believe that our overall goals are fictional ideals we cannot test in reality and that our lives are based on such fictions. What might be the fictional ideal implicit in Bonnie's remark about people not appreciating her, and how might you develop a technique to explore this fictional ideal?

19. We say that a challenge to the leader can be a healthy sign that the group is becoming autonomous. What do you think? How could you differentiate between a challenge and an attack on your leadership?

20. We describe Carolyn as being afraid to get close to people because of childhood injunctions (parental messages). What are some injunctions you received as a child? Are any of your injunctions similar to those of Carolyn? If so, if you were to self-disclose to Carolyn, what might you say? Devise some contracts and homework assignments that you think might encourage Carolyn to challenge her injunctions.

21. Assume that Frances is serious about wanting to lose weight. Do

some reading on behavioral approaches to losing weight, and set up a behavioral plan for her. Include devising specific goals, monitoring behavior, and developing reinforcements. How would you assess the effectiveness of your plan?

22. Imagine how group members might become hostile toward Sam when he says he can't identify with anyone in the group. Describe some possible techniques for working with this situation. If Sam made his remarks at a preliminary session, would you be likely to include him in or exclude him from the group, and why?

23. Your group members say they are stuck and getting nowhere. What are your thoughts about their complaint and about your responsibility for getting them moving?

24. Look at our comments on the various roles leaders may play in conducting groups in the section in which members complain they are stuck and explain your own views on these roles.

25. Jill comments on not feeling safe in her group. If you were a member in a group, what would it require for you to feel safe in it? How might a group leader best work with you on this topic?

26. Jill's statement came during the working stage of a group. The leader focused on her first and then explored the topic with the rest of the group on the hunch that her remark might have been a sign of a groupwide loss of trust. If that were your hunch, how might you explore it?

27. Cheryl says that the real world is not like the group. If you were her group leader and wanted to explain your views on this issue, what would you say? What techniques might be appropriate for bridging gaps between what group and real life are like?

28. As Roz comments, groups can often be seen as focusing on negative emotions. If Roz were to challenge you on this issue, how would you respond? How might you enlist input from people who had expressed a strong emotion such as sadness or anger in your group? How might your own views on this issue affect the way you work in the group?

29. Jane shows a reluctance to cry. Do you think it important for her to cry? Explain.

30. We take the position that we are more concerned with what people do not say, with respect to fears and feelings, than with what they do say in a group. What is your view on this topic?

31. We hold that craziness generally is a choice or something people do rather than something that happens to them. What do you think? You may want to consult the bibliography for some different views on the nature of mental illness.

32. Suppose that you are leading by yourself a group in which several

people are simultaneously expressing intense emotion. How might you react to this situation? What might you do if you were frightened by the intensity of their emotions? How would you most like to be as a leader in this context? Describe a situation in which this phenomenon develops and describe some techniques you might employ.

33. Do you see exploration of dreams as valuable in group work? What reservations, if any, do you have about working with an individual's dream in a group? What techniques would maximize the opportunity for others in the group to be involved in working on one person's dream?

34. How might Melissa's dream about the group be a manifestation of transference, and what techniques might you introduce to explore this possibility?

35. Do some reading on the Gestalt approach to working with dreams. How might you work with Patty's dream and with Melissa's dream using Gestalt methods?

36. What value might there be in asking members to simply share their dreams without attempting to interpret them? What impact might this technique have on group cohesion?

37. What kinds of mistakes might you fear making as a group leader? How might your fear get in the way of your trying new techniques? How might you react to mistakes you make in a group?

38. Your group members believe that a technique you suggested for one of them was a mistake, but you think your suggestion was appropriate. What would you do?

39. We encourage members to gain some intellectual grasp of material they have expressed on an emotional level. We hold that much will be lost if members are not encouraged to think about their work in a group. Many counselors would not agree that putting things into a cognitive framework and attempting to summarize lessons are important. What is your view, and why?

40. Our position is that if you have prepared your group during the initial stage the group will largely take care of itself during the working stage. Do you agree? Why or why not?

CHAPTER SIX

Techniques for
the Final Stage

In this chapter we discuss termination of individual sessions and of the life of the group, an often neglected topic. Leaders often simply and abruptly announce that a group is at an end; they make no attempt to integrate or bring together lessons that could be learned from the group experience. But transfer of learning does not happen automatically; it should be fostered and structured. Indeed, perhaps the two most important phases of a group are its beginning and its end. The beginning, because that is where the tone of the group is set. The end, because that is where there is consolidation of learning.

Avoiding acknowledging a group's termination may reflect an unconscious desire on the part of the leader or members to avoid dealing with the role that endings play in their lives. When termination is not dealt with, the group misses an opportunity to explore an area about which many members have profound feelings. Even more important, much of what clients take away from a group is likely to be lost and forgotten if clients do not make a sustained effort to review and think through the specifics of work they have done.

In general, the following tasks need to be accomplished during the final stage of the group:

- Members can be encouraged to face the inevitable ending of the group and to discuss fully their feelings of separation.

- Members can complete any unfinished business they have with other members or leaders.
- Members can be taught how to leave the group and how to carry with them what they have learned.
- Members can be assisted in making specific plans for change and for taking concrete steps to put the lessons they have learned into effect in their daily lives.
- Leaders can help members discover ways of creating their own support systems after they leave the group.
- Specific plans for follow-up work and evaluation can be made.

Techniques to use in ending a session

The group leader needs to be aware of time. One of the pitfalls of inexperienced therapists is to be unaware of how much time is left in a session. Such leaders may open material up when it would be more valuable to start consolidating what has been accomplished. Their behavior reinforces the tendency of group members to bring up new material at the last minute, (a form of resistance), and it encourages group members to manipulate the leaders into extending the session. It can also lead members to believe that leaders are inadequate or insensitive. For instance, Joan may typically bring up burning issues at the end of the group and then leave complaining of feeling cut off and not listened to or of being left hanging. In the early stages of a group these complaints can set the stage for distrust.

A good practice is to allow at least ten minutes at the end of a session, depending on the size of the group, for members to summarize what the session has meant to them individually. These are some of the kinds of questions they can be asked to answer:

- "Could you briefly summarize what this session has meant to you?"
- "What steps are you willing to take between now and our next session toward making changes in your life?"
- "Was there anything unfinished for you today that you would like to continue in our next meeting?"
- "What was the most important thing you experienced during this meeting?"
- "Could you summarize the important thoughts or insights you may be going away with?"
- "What touched you most in other people's work today?"
- "Before we go, is there any feedback you want to give to someone else here?"

- "What did you learn about yourself?"
- "Is there anything you want to be committed to doing between now and the next time we meet?"
- "Is there anything you regret not working on during this session that you would like to at least mention before we close?"
- "Did you get what you wanted from this session?"
- "Are you satisfied with your level of participation in this session?"
- "If you are apathetic, bored, uninvolved, hostile, resistant, or whatever, what are you willing to do (if anything) to change this attitude?"

This practice of making at least a quick check of every member is extremely important, for it challenges members each week to think about what they are both giving to and getting from the group. If they report that they like what they are experiencing, they can be asked to be specific about what they like and to describe anything they'd like to see done differently. If they report that they are not pleased (with the group itself, the leader, or themselves), then they can be encouraged to be specific both about what they'd want changed and also about their plans for making these changes either in the group or in themselves. If this check is made regularly, members are less likely to complain at the termination of the group that they got nothing from the group and that no attempt was made to enhance work in the group.

What if intense work in a session is not going to be finished by the time the group ends? First, there is nothing inherently terrible or catastrophic about someone's leaving the group with emotions stirred up, although it is important for the person to verbalize the feelings he or she is leaving with. The sensitive leader can help bring a sense of closure simply by acknowledging those feelings still left hanging. Second, people often accomplish more than one might suppose in a fairly short period of time, especially if the leader has let the time constraints be known. People automatically pace their work to the time they know they have.

The leader may tone things down and still give the client something constructive to work with by saying: "I know that there is a lot that has been stirred up in you that we are not going to have time to really work through today. Let me offer a kind of theoretical perspective on what may be going on with what you are exploring so that at least you can go away with some means to think it through a bit more." Another tack at this point is simply to ask the client "Since we are running out of time for exploring this today, would you be willing to try to reflect on it a bit between now and the next meeting and bring it up again then?"

In some situations, leaders may be willing to allow a group to run overtime, but leaders have to be aware of their own limitations. In fairness to the client, they can simply say that at this time they are aware that they have given what they are capable of giving.

Some leaders make the mistake of thinking that unless a concern is brought to a finish that issue is lost forever. However, this is rarely the case. If the issue is an important one, it can easily be returned to again, especially if the member makes a commitment to bring up the issue at the next session when there will be sufficient time to explore it. A leader can remind the client of this commitment at the following meeting by saying: "I remember that during the last session you experienced a lot of intensity related to an issue with your father. I wonder whether you had any more feelings about that or if there is anything you might want to say now to continue with that." Often the client will say: "I don't feel that any more. That's no longer present for me." However, if the client is willing to try to reexperience for a moment what he or she was experiencing during the previous session, without worrying about whether it seems especially here-and-now, the client may well be able to get into those feelings once again.

In a sense, something is always going on at the end of every session. What matters is that whatever is going on be identified and summarized as far as possible. It is unrealistic to think that all members will bring to closure the issues they bring up in a meeting, and it is a mistake to attempt premature closure on an issue. Leaders should be careful to avoid fixing up a member's problem largely because of the leaders' hope that everyone leave happy and complete. It is often constructive for clients to leave with a sense of incompleteness, something to think about after the session and to work with in future sessions. If people leave feeling too comfortable, they may not be motivated to reflect on what occurred in the session.

One technique for closing a session and linking it to the next is to have members announce homework assignments or some means of carrying further the work they did in a session and then to report on these assignments at the beginning of the next session. Homework assignments can be devised by the members themselves, by the leader or by other members of the group. Too often members do little thinking about or working on a personal issue they explored during a session unless they commit themselves to doing so. For example, if Frank is fearful of dealing with his professors, he can commit himself to seeking out a professor before the next session and talking with the professor about his fears in the class. If Frank takes the ultimate responsibility for deciding on the nature of his assignment, he is already taking steps toward change.

Leaders can make a practice of giving their reactions, a group-process commentary, and a summary of the meeting toward the end of the session. They might comment on the cohesion of the group, the degree to which members freely brought up topics for work, the willingness of members to take risks and talk about unsafe topics, the degree to which members interacted with one another (as opposed to speaking only directly to and through the leader), and the willingness of members to discuss negative concerns or feelings. Leaders might also write notes about each session during the week and then use these comments at the beginning of the next session as a catalyst for linking sessions. Members can also write down at the end of each session specific topics, questions, concerns, problems, or personal issues that they'd be willing to talk about in the next session. They are thus encouraged to think before the next session about what they've committed themselves to bring up. Although some therapists may think that this practice is too forced or planned, it is one technique for confronting members with their responsibility to use the limited time available to them in a group to its fullest. Another way to close each session is to set aside the last five minutes for members to fill out a brief assessment or rating sheet. These assessments give the leaders an ongoing sense of how members are perceiving the group. The rating sheets can be tallied up in a few minutes, and the results can be presented at the beginning of the next session, especially if trends are noted. A rating scale from 1 to 10 can be used. Members can rate themselves, other members, and the leaders on some of the following dimensions (the leaders might fill out these forms too):

- To what degree were you involved in this session?
- To what degree did you want to be in the group today?
- To what degree did you see yourself as an active, contributing member of the group today?
- To what degree were you willing to take risks in the group?
- To what degree did you trust other members in the group today?
- To what degree did you trust the group leader today?
- To what degree has today's session stimulated you to think about your problems, your life situation, or possible decisions you might want to make?
- To what degree did today's group touch you emotionally or help you to recall emotion-laden events in your life?
- To what degree did you care about other members in this session?
- To what degree were you willing to share what you were feeling and thinking in the session today?
- To what degree did you have clear goals for this session?

- To what degree are you willing to actively practice some new behavior this week?
- At this point, to what degree are you eager to return to the group next week?
- To what degree did you prepare yourself or think about this session before you came today?
- To what degree do you see the group as being alive, goal directed, and energetic?
- To what degree do you think the group is cohesive and together at this time?
- To what degree are you willing to give others in the group feedback?
- To what degree are you willing to nondefensively take in the feedback you receive and consider it carefully?
- To what degree do you see this group as a positive force in helping you make the changes in your life that you want to make?
- To what degree did you see the group as productive today?

If leaders tally up the results and see clear trends such as a lack of involvement, a low level of risk taking, an absence of trust, a limited amount of sharing, resistance to returning to the group, and an absence of cohesion, they can open the next session with a remark such as this one: "For the past two weeks most of you have apparently seen this group as a place where you don't feel safe to reveal personal material. Many of you agree that caring is absent, that goals are unclear, and that the energy level of the group is low. I'd like to have us look at this trend and see what we want to do about this situation, especially since we have a number of group sessions left." The members can then bring out some of their perceptions and openly evaluate the group, and the members and leaders can make decisions about changing the group's direction.

In summary, if leaders lose sight of the approaching end of a session, they have no choice but to abruptly announce "Well, group, we've run out of time; see you next week." If this practice becomes the norm, there is no closure for a session, no evaluation of accountability, and no concrete planning for the upcoming session.

Techniques to use in terminating a group

Preparing for termination. In closed groups with a fixed life span, the issue of termination must be faced well before the last session. Group members should be encouraged to express their feelings about the group's ending and to identify what more they want to do before the opportunity is gone. If the group is cohesive, members also need to deal with the sense of loss they may feel when the group is over.

When the end of the group is still a fair time away, the fact that an end will come can be used to motivate people to work. Indeed, with marathons and residential groups, leaders can point out that the time will pass quickly and that the experience will soon be over; members cannot assume that they have plenty of time for getting around to doing what they want to do.

Leaders can use questions such as these to prompt members to work: "Assume that this is the last chance you are going to have in this group to explore what you want. How do you want to use this time?" "If this were the last session of this group, how would you feel about what you have done, and what would you wish you had done differently?"

In addition, as the end of the group approaches, and preferably not at the last meeting, members can explore feelings they may have about the ending of the group and parallels in their lives with separations and death. Leaders should not underestimate the likelihood that the group has become for several of the participants a powerful family symbol or a symbol of hope and of the possibility for change. They should have ample opportunity to explore these associations.

Leaders should also be alert to signs that the members are avoiding dealing with the group's ending. When members start introducing topics they worked on long before, when the work in the group seems lacking in intensity, when there is much lateness, joking, or intellectualizing, members may be signaling through such resistance their unwillingness to leave. The leaders' own willingness to initiate the topic of termination can be excellent modeling here.

Reviewing highlights of the group experience.   Much of what members learn in a group will be lost unless certain devices are used to help them recall these lessons and to apply what they've learned in their everyday lives. One such device is to ask members to spontaneously recall moments they shared together: "I'd like each of you to close your eyes and imagine all the events of the time we've been together. Let yourself imagine that you have these events on videotape, that you can play back these tapes and actually see and remember what occurred in the group. Now, let yourself go back to our very first session, and for a few minutes just sit with your eyes closed and see whatever comes to you about this first session. What do you remember feeling at that initial session? How did people look to you then?" After a couple of minutes the leader can ask members to freely and randomly share glimpses of what they remember of this early session. Then the leader can say: "Now close your eyes again and for a few minutes sit in silence and just let this tape go through your mind. Let whatever comes to mind get sharper and more focused. Remember whatever stands out for you. What were some of the events that you recall most clearly and that had the most meaning for you? Whenever you feel ready, just let yourself speak and share with the rest of us what you are remembering."

This technique of recalling special moments may bring back to life incidents of conflict in the group, of closeness and warmth, of humor and lightness, of pain, of tension and anxiety. The more members can verbalize their experiences and the more they can recall of what actually happened in the group, the greater their chances of integrating and using the lessons they have learned.

Fred, for example, says: "I'm thinking about the time when the members in here told me that although I appeared tough they saw a tender side of me deep down. That helped me a great deal to feel okay about *having feelings*, although I must admit that I still have a ways to go before I feel okay about expressing these feelings openly." Sue mentions the time that she confronted the group leader and relates: "I can still feel myself shaking as I let myself get angry at you. That was a new feeling for me to feel *and* to express my anger to authority figures, and I learned that the world doesn't fall apart when I do get angry." Barbara recalls: "In one session there was this heavy silence in the room, which felt terribly uncomfortable to me. I wanted to say something to break the tension in the room. It was important for me to see that the feelings and reactions we were keeping to ourselves were preventing us from going anywhere. I learned that conflict that isn't brought out into the open doesn't magically disappear. And I saw that expressing this conflict was all right."

By allowing every member to share significant moments and significant lessons, this technique helps bring the entire group experience back to all the members. People have a chance to see how their work had an influence on others. The leader can help the conceptualization process by asking members what they learned about themselves and others during these significant moments. Although this technique of recalling and sharing events takes only a few minutes, it can be a special time and a valuable experience.

Exploring the issue of separation.   Members commonly feel resistance to leaving a group in which they've developed genuine bonds of intimacy and in which they can be themselves without fear of rejection. They often are concerned that they will not be as open and trusting with people outside the group. They wonder whether they will experience the same closeness, caring, nonjudgmental atmosphere, and support once they leave the group. Although leaders cannot deny the importance of recognizing and exploring the feelings of members about separation, they can also encourage members to look for ways they might find support in their relationships outside the group. Leaders might remind group members that the closeness they value in the group did not happen by accident. Members need to recognize what they did to create this special climate; they need to recall that they made a commitment to create an effective group and that they initiated trust. They can then consider how to continue reaching out in similar ways in everyday situations.

Rehearsing new roles.   Role-playing techniques can be extremely effective in giving people a chance to practice new behaviors. They can receive feedback from others in the group on the impact they might have, and other members can provide alternative behaviors they may not have thought of.

A common mistake of some participants is to focus on how they might change others in their lives, rather than focusing on what they might change about themselves. Leaders can stress that members have the power to change themselves but they cannot directly change others. For example, in the group Al became aware that he holds most of his feelings of both anger and tenderness within himself. Through the group, he learned that expressing feelings was not unmanly and that terrible consequences didn't follow when he did express himself. Al is now concerned for his children, whom he sees as holding in their feelings. During a role rehearsal he lectures his children about the benefits of expressing emotions. In their feedback the other members remind Al that his children are more likely to begin to express their emotions if he expresses his own emotions to them rather than telling them why they should do so.

Some members also become impatient with the significant people in their lives, wanting them to share the level of awareness they have arrived at through their group experience. They forget that they had to work to achieve that awareness. After they role-play the situations they expect to encounter, other members may remind them that their impatience and insistence on instant change will push people away.

Another common pitfall for people leaving a group is that they often come to rely on group jargon. Even within the group people may lose a full awareness of their concerns when they rely too much on expressions like "staying with your feelings," "projecting," and "getting away from 'shoulds'." And members are likely to alienate people outside the group if they use such language. Role playing conversations they intend to have with others can help them overcome this tendency.

Being specific about outcomes and plans.   During all group sessions members can avoid general and global statements and instead can be specific and descriptive. During the final stage of a group, being specific is especially important if members are to be clear about what they learned about themselves and how they are going to apply these lessons. If a member says "This group has been very good for me; I've learned a lot and grown a lot," the leader's response might be: "Specifically, what did you learn, and how did you see yourself as growing? In what ways has this group been good for you? What are some things that have been good for you?" If members are specific both about what they have learned and about their plans for change, the likelihood that they will act to change their behavior is increased.

Feedback during the final stage also needs to be specific. Members can be discouraged from categorizing others as they give feedback and from saying something they've not said to others before in the group, especially something negative. Introducing new material is not helpful at this time when the point is to consolidate what has already been seen. A final feedback session is not an opportunity to blast someone or to hit and run, nor is it the time to shower someone with such global sweetness that the person has a hyperglycemic reaction! The purpose of the final feedback session is rather to give members specific tools they can take away and use. Here, specific reactions, impressions, and brief comments are valuable. One technique is to ask the people receiving feedback not to respond but to listen carefully to what is being said. Their silence does not imply that they accept the feedback as valid; it simply helps them to consider what they hear more seriously than they might if they were to give an immediate response.

Another feedback procedure is to ask members to finish some of the following incomplete statements for each participant:

- "My fear for you is . . . ."
- "My hope for you is . . . ."
- "What I'd like for you to remember most is . . . ."
- "One thing I like best about you is . . . ."
- "One thing that distances you from me is . . . ."
- "A way I see you as blocking your strengths is . . . ."

Another member can write down the comments for each person receiving feedback and then give the person these notes. Or members can write down their sentence completions and then give them to each participant. This procedure makes forgetting these comments less likely.

Summarizing personal reactions to the group.   During the last session of a group it's valuable for members to make at least brief statements about what it was like for them to be members of the group and to summarize what they are taking with them as a result of the experience. Again, the rationale is that members will carry away more information from a group if they verbalize their reactions and give meaning and perspective to what they've learned. Here are some examples of questions members might address:

- "What has it been like for you to be a member of this group? What have you liked or disliked about being in this group?"
- "What have you learned about yourself? What did you learn about how others view you?"
- "What were some of the major turning points in this group for you? What were a few of the most significant events for you in this group?"
- "What are some of the things you most want to say as this group is closing?"

This technique allows all members to have some idea of what each person is taking away from the group. It also encourages members to think through and to pull together the lessons they have learned.

Projecting the future.   In using this technique, the leader asks members to think of the changes they'd most like to have made six months hence, one year hence, and five years hence. Members can then imagine that the entire group is meeting at one of these designated times and they can say what they'd most want to say to the others at that time. They can also state what they will have to do to accomplish these goals. This device gets members focused on the changes they'd like to make in their lives on a short-term and a long-range basis.

Members sometimes express the fear that they will not change. Here a useful technique is to ask them to imagine meeting again one year later and to express their feelings about changes they didn't make. "How do you feel about continuing pretty much as you were a year ago, when the group ended?"

Making contracts.   Making contracts for further action once the group ends can be a valuable way to help members try new behaviors in their day-to-day living. One technique is to ask members to bring a written statement of a change they are willing to make once the group ends. Participants can read their contracts aloud, and others can give specific suggestions for implementing the contracts and can comment on the degree to which the contracts seem realistic.

David, for example, has come to realize through his group work that he consistently puts himself down with self-defeating remarks and does not try new activities for fear of failure. He knows he sets himself up for failure with his internal dialogue. He decides that he wants to change this behavior by attempting new projects. He lists several of these projects and asks the group to suggest how he can avoid slipping back into his old ways. As a result of their suggestions, he agrees as part of his contract to make several signs and tape them to the mirror in his bathroom, to the refrigerator door, and in other places in the house. The signs read: "I have a right to ask for what I want." "I don't have to continue to set myself up for defeat." "I can and will do more than I've told myself I could do in the past."

Learning not to discount or forget.   Members tend to forget what they've learned in a group or to discount the insights they've had. After the termination of a group, members may discount the value of what they experienced in the group, primarily by telling themselves that the group experience cannot be replicated in everyday life. For example, Loretta convinces herself that people in the group were just being kind to her and that she cannot find the same support for making changes now that she has left the group.

In the discounting exercise, several members form an inner circle and talk with each other as if they were meeting several months after termination of the group. They talk particularly about all the ways in which they might lessen the value of the group and discount the experience. The rationale here is to give members a chance to foresee the internal dialogue they might engage in as time moves on. Alternatively, they can role-play how they might depreciate their group experience when describing it to people in their everyday lives. If members are thus confronted with the likelihood of forgetting and discounting, they are less likely to do so.

Techniques to use after terminating a group

Conducting follow-up interviews.   As a safety check and as a method of assessment, leaders can try to arrange a private interview with each group member a few weeks to a few months after the group terminates. Such an interview can be beneficial to the client as a booster shot and to the leaders as a way to evaluate the effectiveness of the group.

The purpose of this session is to determine the degree to which members have met their personal goals and fulfilled their contracts. It's a chance for both leaders and members to discuss the impact of the group, to talk about specific ways of continuing whatever learning was begun, and to discuss any unfinished business or feelings left over from the group. If members are having problems applying what they learned in the group to everyday life, this individual contact is an opportunity to explore ways of dealing with these difficulties. It is also an excellent opportunity for leaders to suggest other groups or individual counseling if they seem appropriate.

Encouraging contact with other members.   A technique that can lend support to members as they are practicing new behavior or completing an action program is to contact another member from the group periodically after termination. This contact can be especially important when members find that they are not pushing themselves to do much now that the group is finished. By calling another member and reporting on their progress or lack of it, they can gain both support and stimulation. Members can select one or more persons with whom they are willing to make contact for at least a few months after termination to report progress toward their goals. This is a method of accountability, and it is a way for people to learn how to establish a support system.

Arranging a follow-up session.   A follow-up session can take place a couple of months after the end of the group to assess the impact of the group on each of the members. Having such a session is one more way of maximizing the chance that members will receive lasting benefit from the group experience. Because members know that they will meet to review what they've done with the group at some future time, they are likely to stick to their contracts. Such a session also provides a chance for them to acknowledge how the lessons they learned fit their lives, and the leader can get a sense of the overall impact of the group.

Learning where to go for further growth.   A group experience may be just the beginning of growth for many of the members. Even though some members may appear to get little from their first group, it often readies them for future growth experiences. Thus, during the final session, the follow-up interview, or the follow-up session, leaders might give a number of suggestions to those participants who wish to continue the work they've begun. These suggestions may include specific recommendations for individual counseling and therapy and recommendations for other closed groups, workshops, or perhaps an ongoing group with some of the same members from the group that just terminated. Leaders can also suggest reading material and perhaps organizations that members can contact for a variety of social activities. The members themselves might use part of the final session to brainstorm about ways of going further with their work. Because members may be ready to consider another group or individual counseling only after some time has elapsed, the follow-up session is an excellent place to reinforce the value of getting involved in various types of growth projects.

Techniques to use in evaluating the group

Evaluation form. Leaders can use some type of assessment device to determine the outcomes of a group. We favor devices that tap the subjective reactions of the members both at the final session and at the follow-up session. There is often a significant difference in how members feel about a group immediately after it ends and how they feel several months later. Feedback in both instances is valuable.

An evaluation form can ask members to assess their degree of satisfaction with the group and the level of investment they had in it; it can ask members to recall highlights or significant events; it can ask them to specify actions they took during the group to make desired changes; it can ask them to state what techniques were most and least helpful and to give suggestions for changing the format; or it can ask them to describe how the group appeared through their eyes. Depending on the membership, a structured check list might be devised or an open-ended letter might be asked for, or a combination of a rating scale and essay questions might be used.

Not only is this evaluation procedure valuable as a way for leaders to measure the effectiveness of the group, but this procedure is valuable as a way for the members to focus their thinking on what they did during the group and what they received from the experience.

The questionnaire in the box is one evaluation form that leaders can use to get some idea of the impact of the group on the members.

MEMBER EVALUATION FORM

1. What general effect has your group experience had on your life?
2. What were the highlights of the group experience for you?

3. What specific things did you become aware of about yourself—about your lifestyle, attitudes, and relationships with others?
4. What changes have you made in your life that you can attribute at least partially to your group experience?
5. Which of the techniques used by the group leaders had the most impact on you? Which techniques had the least impact?
6. What are some of your perceptions of the group leaders and their styles?
7. What kinds of problems did you encounter in the outside world when you tried to implement some of the decisions you made in the group?
8. What are some of the questions you have asked yourself since the group ended?
9. Did the group experience have any negative effects on you?
10. How did your participation in the group affect significant people in your life?
11. How might your life be different had you not been a member of the group?
12. If you had to say in a sentence or two what the group meant to you, how would you respond?

___

Group leader's journal. Keeping a process journal is an excellent technique for leaders to use in evaluating the progress of a group and in assessing changes in the group during the stages of its development. Leaders can focus not only on what occurs within the group and on the members' behaviors but also on their own reactions. Here are some areas leaders might write about:

• How did you initially view the group? What were your reactions to the group as a whole?
• What were some initial reactions you had to each member? How did any of these reactions or impressions change? What members did you find yourself most wanting to work with? What members did you have difficulty with?
• How did you feel in leading this group? Did you generally want to be in the group? Did you take your share of responsibility for the group's progress?
• What turning points did you see in this group?
• What factors do you see as contributing to the success or the failure of the group?
• What techniques did you use and what were the outcomes?

- What were the key events of each session?
- Describe the dynamics of the group and the relationships among members.

By keeping such a journal you can review trends in the group and devise changes in format or techniques for future groups.

You might also type up your observations of each session and give these notes to the members prior to the next session. Members too can be encouraged to keep brief process journals, and both you and the members can share your observations. At termination, these journals provide a summary of significant events in the group. In addition, when coleaders meet to discuss the group's progress, they can refer to their process notes for any differences in perceptions.

Finally, this journal is a good device for generating personal work for you as a leader. You can reserve a section of the journal for writing down whatever comes to mind about unresolved problems in your life. For example, if you become aware of hurt feelings and rejection through the work of some members, you may choose not to work on that problem in the group itself but can profit from writing in your journal about further work that you might do in your own therapy.

Concluding comments

In this chapter we have emphasized the importance of ending a given session and terminating a group in such a way as to maximize learning and provide an opportunity for growth and change. Reviewing highlights, consolidating lessons, role playing, getting and giving feedback, and writing are all useful techniques during the final stage. A group will not promote insight or growth if the leader fails to pay sufficient attention to its ending phases or if the leader emphasizes just the experiential dimension of the group process without enlisting the intellects of members to give meaning to what they have experienced.

QUESTIONS AND ACTIVITIES

1. Suppose that your group is almost at the end of a session and several people introduce new and potent material. What might you say or do in response? Can you think of any ways in which you may have set the members up to introduce new material at the end?
2. Describe some techniques or strategies you might employ to wrap up a particular session of a group.
3. We state that not acknowledging a group's termination may reflect an unconscious desire on the part of the leaders or members to

avoid dealing with separation and endings. How might your own feelings and reactions toward the termination of a group that you are leading affect the manner in which members fully explore their own feelings about the group's termination?

4. Describe what you regard as the most important gains from group work and how the ending of a session can enhance these gains. Discuss variables such as the population and the stated purpose of the group.

5. What value do you see in homework assignments and other suggestions for action that are designed to give members practice in new behavior outside group sessions? What techniques of this kind might you use in one of your groups?

6. Suppose a member of your group comments on your looking at your watch. What might you say? As a group leader, do you pay attention to time and do you allow sufficient time at the end of a session for a summary and integration of what took place? What are some techniques that you might employ in this regard?

7. When and how might you reintroduce material that a member of your group worked on in a previous session? What are some important considerations here? Would you remind a member of something she seemed to have left unfinished at the prior session? If she indicates that she could no longer get into it, then what?

8. What are some factors you would consider in assessing the progress of a group you were leading?

9. At the last meeting of a ten-week group, several members urge you to extend the group for a few weeks more. What theoretical considerations seem significant to you in this situation? How would you deal with this matter?

10. The group has come to an end, and a member expresses an interest in continuing in a social relationship with you. What considerations do you think are especially important here?

11. We discuss some techniques for having members of the group review significant moments in the group's history. Invent some similar techniques of your own, and imagine how they might go.

12. A supervisor asks you how your group is going. What criteria would you use in making your reply?

13. We suggest some questions to use on an assessment form for having members evaluate a given session. Write an assessment form that would be suitable for a group you might lead. Why would you or wouldn't you use such a form?

14. What are the most important considerations during the final stage of a group? What specific issues would you want members of your

group to focus on during this phase, and what techniques could you use to help them do so?

15. A member plans to leave a group that will continue to meet. How do you see this sort of termination as different from the termination of the whole group? What issues are different?

16. Members cannot possibly remember everything they experience in a group. What would you most hope that participants would remember, and what techniques might you use to help them recall and review these lessons?

17. What negative consequences do you think there might be if members do not deal explicitly with the fact that the group is ending? What techniques might you use if you sense participants are inclined to avoid talking about the group's termination?

18. Toward the end of a group you ask the members to talk about what they have gained from the experience. One of them says: "I really have gotten a lot from this. I've experienced a lot, and I've gotten in touch with my feelings. It was great!" Would you have any concerns about this person's remarks, and what might you say to him?

19. We state that transfer of learning from the group to everyday life does not happen automatically—that it should be fostered and structured. What are your thoughts on this topic? What techniques would facilitate transferring what was learned in the group to other situations?

20. Imagine planning with a colleague or a fellow student strategies to use during the final few sessions before your group ends. If you are opposed to planning strategies in advance, explain why.

21. Your group is holding a follow-up session several months after its termination. What kinds of questions would you most want to ask the participants? What do you see as the significant goals of this meeting?

22. Follow-up sessions may lead participants to feel guilty about progress they have not made. What techniques could you use to enhance gains people did make?

23. You suggest to a participant that another group or individual counseling might be a good idea for her. She says she feels you are telling her that she has failed to get anything from your group. What might you say to her? What referrals might you make or what ideas for further group or individual counseling might you suggest to members in general?

24. We talk about the value for group leaders of keeping an ongoing journal in which they write process notes as well as describe their

personal reactions. What value do you see such a journal having in helping you to assess a group's progress? What specific topics do you think you'd most want to include in your process journal? Discuss.

CHAPTER SEVEN

In a Nutshell

In this chapter we isolate and highlight a series of points that we have only touched on earlier when addressing another topic or that clarify some of the underlying principles of our style of leadership.

Recognize the primacy of the client. In this book we may have seemed more directive and structured in our leadership style than is really the case. Perhaps that impression was unavoidable, given that the book is about techniques. Although we take an active role in leading, we see ourselves as constantly responding to and seeking to flow with our clients. We see therapy as a kind of dance: sometimes we lead and sometimes we follow, but in either case we seek to be aware of how we can best move with our partners. We believe that sensitivity to and respect for the client are fundamental to the therapeutic interaction. We seek to suit techniques to the client rather than molding the client to our needs and our techniques.

Use techniques as means, not ends. We believe that techniques are no better than the person using them and no good at all if not sensitively adapted to the particular client and context. The outcome of the use of a technique is affected by the climate of the group and by the relationship between the therapist and the client. Techniques are a means to an end—they amplify material that is present and encourage exploration of where that material leads. When leaders become more concerned with techniques than with their capacity to dance with their clients, when techniques become ends in themselves, then the heart of group process has been lost.

Cultivate the soil. We do not believe that techniques should be sprung on group members or be imposed without regard for the degree to which a relationship with group members has been cultivated. Particularly with techniques that evoke intense emotion, we seek to gauge the readiness of the client to work with us and with the exercise we propose. We do not command. We invite clients to experiment and leave room for them to disagree; we believe that we have to earn their trust by demonstrating our good will.

Use tentative language. We characteristically introduce a technique by saying "I wonder whether you would be willing to . . .," "How would it be if you . . .," or "Do you suppose you could . . . ." When we offer an interpretation, we typically begin by saying "I have a hunch that . . ." or "If I were you I might feel that . . . ." We try in our choice of words not to give the impression that we are pronouncing unimpeachable diagnoses from on high. We do not, however, water our words down with meaningless qualifiers. Our own confrontive feedback, for example, we give in an especially direct and unqualified way. But in providing interpretations and in introducing techniques we employ tentative language that gives the client room to gracefully decline.

Use simple and direct language. We introduce techniques so simply and clearly that a child could understand the instructions. Groups inevitably develop their own special language and metaphors, but we tend to discourage using overworked popular expressions, psychobabble, and encounter-group clichés like "getting in touch with your feelings"; we use language that is clear and descriptive.

Be aware of nonverbal communication. We seek to be aware of the nonverbal communication of the client and of how we nonverbally present ourselves to the group. In order to establish a trusting relationship, not only our choice of words but also the clues we provide about our attitudes toward clients communicate a basic respect for the people we work with.

Be ready to abandon a technique. A drop in the energy level of a group is often an indication that a technique is not working. One of us was conducting a session in which a client spoke of his loneliness. Others in the group were invited to form an inner circle and talk about their feelings of loneliness. It quickly became evident that the inner circle was listless, and the rest of the group was restless. We are willing in such instances to recognize stale water and move on.

Don't fight the river. We may sometimes introduce a technique with a preconceived idea of what is going to happen, but the material that emerges may lead in quite a different direction. Or a client may misunderstand our directions and do something quite different from what we had in mind. We also find that a technique may work well once or many times, but we can't always count on its working the same way twice. In all these instances we don't fight the river.

Be willing to experiment. We believe that in some ways the difference between an experienced and an inexperienced leader lies in the willingness to experiment and to forge ahead. We find that we can't draw on our capacity for spontaneously utilizing our own emotional resources if we are afraid to experiment in creating techniques to fit a context. We teach beginning group leaders to be aware of certain pitfalls and to take necessary precautions, but we equally seek to encourage them to trust themselves. If you find yourself becoming stale or uncreative, you might consider getting more supervision, working more with different coleaders, or attending different sorts of workshops as a participant.

Realize that therapy is necessary for oneself. We believe that, for the therapist, exploring one's own life should be a long-term commitment. We think that we probably cannot, and, in any case should not, take our clients any further than we ourselves are willing to go. To some degree we find that our own therapy deepens and progresses as a consequence of leading, but we believe it important to make periodic efforts to explore ourselves further. One interesting way to gauge the progress of your own therapy to date is to ask yourself these questions: "Realistically, what would a group be like if it were composed of members whose personalities were like mine? Where would such a group bog down? What kinds of resistance would commonly emerge in it?"

Link the work of clients. We believe that, for exercises to be genuinely group techniques, they generally ought to allow for several members of the group to work at the same time. Some individual work in a group setting can be fine, but involving several persons better utilizes time and resources. In this area the leader orchestrates the group using creativity and intuition to identify common themes from the information clients have provided and to indicate how members can work together on these themes.

Use props. We find that techniques can be considerably enriched if we pay attention to useful items in the immediate environment. A leader working with a client who spoke of feeling boxed in remembered seeing a large cardboard box just outside. After the box was brought into the room, the client got inside and spoke about the various things he felt closed him in. Such employment of props can enhance techniques that seek to magnify an experience and can provide clients with valuable symbols in their subsequent reflections.

Use humor. We often have been struck by how clients can laugh about topics they were crying over only a few minutes before. We have also found that humor and laughter often spontaneously break out in a group. Far from causing a group to avoid a topic, humor often serves to solidify insight. We don't hesitate to have fun and to make humor part of the techniques we introduce. For example, humor can be used to give feedback. One female member of a group was unable to understand—so she said—why men so often made passes at her. The male leader later appeared wearing a low-cut suitably padded blouse, and tight shorts: he paraded around the room in a perfect imitation of her, saying "Why do you all make passes at me?" The performance was hilarious, and the client was able to receive feedback in this form that she had not been able to take in before. At this point in the group the level of trust and the work already accomplished made this interaction feasible. Even more important, the leader was able to imitate the client in a way that communicated that the humor was caring and not introduced at the client's expense. For genuine and constructive humor to be used in a group we find there has to be a strong level of trust.

Put aside prejudices and assumptions. If we want to be therapeutic agents, we find we must put aside our preconceived notions about the people we are working with. We do not try to force work with clients into the mold of our theories and interpretations. And we also try not to see clients in terms of stereotypes and generalizations. If you are working with adolescents and introduce a technique that assumes they feel rebellious or if you are working with the elderly and introduce a technique that assumes they are no longer sexual, you impose your preconceived notions rather than allowing the clients to tell you who they are. Minimally, we would hope that you acknowledge your prejudices to yourself, and as far as possible keep them out of the therapy session.

Be aware of values. We have said that techniques both are an extension of the therapist and are created to fit the context and the character of the client. We do not believe it possible for our own values, which are a part of our character, to be excluded from influencing the material we pursue and the techniques we suggest. Inevitably, in our groups, when we suggest a technique we imply the direction in which we want group members to try to go. When we propose a new behavior, we imply that this behavior is one we hope our clients might incorporate. For example, if we encourage a client to role-play striking up a conversation with a member of the opposite sex, we are hoping that the client can learn to be more comfortable doing so. The fact that our techniques reflect our values does not mean that we impose our values on the group. The fact that we have hopes for how our clients might be does not mean we do not respect them for reaching their own decisions. Generally, we take our cues from what our clients indicate they want for themselves. Where our own values come into play, we feel that at least we can be aware of them in ourselves. If a value of yours is that conflict should be avoided at all costs, then you are likely to introduce techniques that bypass conflict. If a value of yours is that anger should be expressed often, then you are likely to introduce techniques that accentuate anger. Minimally, you can be aware of your preferences and can make yourself and your values known to clients; that way you are not as likely to use your preferences to manipulate others.

Go with the obvious. Although we may use complex interpretations as a way of thinking about our clients, we want to work with what is present and obvious. So often leaders go digging and ignore what is before their eyes. They strain to interpret what a lot of restlessness means and fail to simply encourage people to say what is going on. Jennifer picks Henry to role-play her lover, and the leaders fail to pick up on the fact that she finds Henry attractive. A technique should accentuate what is obvious.

Think about theory. We believe that group leaders should continually rethink their theoretical orientations. A theory is a cognitive map, but not a fixed map; our theories about how we work are open to modifications based on experience. At any given time we are able to say how we are viewing human nature and how this view affects our style of therapy, our rationale for introducing the techniques we do, and our vision of what we think we have to offer clients. Many practitioners have a high regard for their intuitions and hunches but an aversion to the intellect and an unwillingness to reflect on what they are doing. If techniques are to be extensions of the therapist's character, therapists must be willing to frequently review their theoretical assumptions.

Recognize the limits of responsibility. We see the therapeutic partnership as a shared examination of our lives, our feelings, our possibilities for being different. Earlier we used the metaphor of therapy as a dance, where the therapist sometimes leads, sometimes follows, but always seeks to go with the shared movement. We do not believe we have sole responsibility for the success of the dance. We see our responsibilities primarily as preparing ourselves and our members for the group experience, providing a context in which meaningful work is likely to occur, making ourselves available for hearing and encountering our clients, providing skills and techniques that facilitate the explorations of the group, and seeking to maximize the opportunity to learn from the experience. We do not believe that if a group goes well it is all to our credit or that if a group is unproductive it is all our fault. We join with our clients in a dance and share the responsibility for its performance.

Don't attempt to change people directly. We assume that our clients may change profoundly under our influence, but we don't see these changes as something we do to them as if they, like the sculptor's clay, were the passive recipients of our technical manipulations. We do not think people's lives simply and passively undergo transformation as a result of what we do. We seek to provide an optimal environment or context within which group participants can express what they feel, reexamine and rethink decisions they have made, try out new behavior, and, in short, consider ways they could change. Although a technique we introduce can invite participants to change and encourage them to do so, we do not think it is the technique that brings the change about; the technique simply enhances the client's awareness of the possibility of being different. Once the client is aware of these options, the hardest work begins as the client attempts to carry what has been learned into daily life. Consequently, we are interested in techniques not simply as vehicles for expressing emotion but as enhancers of thinking, of examining assumptions, of trying out different behaviors, and of practicing ways of being different.

Attempt to integrate thinking and feeling and doing. We do not accept a radical gap between thinking and feeling and behaving. When we encourage group members to express how they feel, we are asking them to look at how they spontaneously think and thus at how they provide the framework for the way they act. If at certain times, we request clients to refrain from thinking about what they are saying, our goal is to have them eventually think clearly and be in a position to change. Some theories of therapy emphasize feeling as opposed to thinking; some stress thinking rather than feeling; and some accentuate behavior independently of thinking or feeling. Our style of leadership and the techniques we employ show our disagreement with these polarities and divisions. We seek through our use of techniques to give our clients an opportunity to experience and express their emotions. But we are also concerned to have them reflect on how their feelings connect with their belief systems, the assumptions they make, and the early decisions on which these assumptions may be based. Then we encourage them to try out different ways of behaving within the group and, lastly, to consider ways of carrying concrete behavioral changes into their lives outside the group.

Encourage verbalization. A great many of our techniques emphasize verbal behavior: verbal role playing, sentence completions, go-arounds. This emphasis fits with our theoretical commitment to thinking, feeling, and doing as a package because what we say reveals how we think, feel, and act. Typically, when we ask group members to say something, our hope is to promote their talking spontaneously and unguardedly. Contrary to popular group jargon, we are not exactly seeking to have our clients "get out of their heads" or "turn off their intellects"; we are asking them to refrain from being too guarded. By the same token, talking differently is one way of being different. Techniques that ask clients to say something different explore the possibility of change, pointing to how they could feel, think, and act.

Explore polarities. To achieve our goal of integrating thinking and feeling and doing, we seek to acknowledge and work with polarities in our clients. All clients have opposite sides within them, even though they often do not want to acknowledge or own them: a thinking side versus a feeling side, being like one parent versus being like the other, being dependent versus being independent, being passive versus being active, being trusting versus being suspicious, being open versus being closed. Many of our techniques ask group members to exaggerate one side of themselves (whether owned or disowned) in order to stay with it long enough to get more data about it and to decide whether it is a way they want to be. Our techniques do not aim at getting rid of one side. Rather, we find that having clients acknowledge various sides of themselves through techniques that emphasize polarities is a prelude to their accepting parts of themselves they needlessly reject, rejecting parts they needlessly continue to accept, and considering possibilities for integrated change.

Work with the past, present, and future. Some group leaders think of their groups as having a present, or here-and-now, orientation, while others focus on the past. In a way, one of our biggest concerns is to generate techniques that focus on the future, on how one could be. However, the groundwork for change is getting clients clear about who they are now, based on their personal histories. Our techniques move back and forth among all three temporal frames of reference. Typically, we begin with current concerns introduced by group members and with dynamics we currently see in the group. We assume that present material is rooted in childhood lessons, but when we introduce techniques that focus on the past we seek to use only material that can be made experientially present. "What do you want to say to your father now that you didn't say then?" "Could you exaggerate a part of you as you are now that you learned from your mother as a child?" We avoid exploring past history in an abstract and detached way; we seek to examine the relevance of the past by reliving it now and connecting it with current struggles. The point of such techniques is to put clients into a position to choose how they want to be now in light of their beginnings.

Be aware of the ethical context. We believe that leaders should consider the ethical dimensions of using techniques in groups. There are risks involved in groups and risks specifically related to group techniques. These risks can be minimized. Leaders should adequately prepare and inform group members. Techniques should be genuinely geared to further the goals of the members rather than being artificially imposed. Leaders should not hide behind techniques as if what they had to offer were a technical bag of tricks. While being creative and willing to experiment, leaders should base techniques in their theories of group work and in what they have been willing to explore within themselves.

Realize the importance of preparation. We believe that leaders should prepare themselves and group members for the group experience. Adequate preparation reduces the risks of group work and maximizes effectiveness. Much of what goes wrong in some groups and much of what accounts for why they never reach an effective working stage can be traced to the lack of an adequate foundation. Preparation includes informing potential members about the nature of the group, teaching them about how they might get the most from a group experience, and encouraging them to focus on the specific issues and concerns they wish to explore. Leader preparation is relevant too. You can get yourself psychologically ready for a group by taking time to reflect on your own life and to think about your objectives for the group. Preparing with a coleader whom you can learn from and who complements your own style can be ideal.

Enhance the initial stage. The techniques we use at the start of a group are fairly structured and have the purpose of clarifying goals and of working with the predictable material of the initial stage. We introduce techniques for setting individual goals and for working with such issues as distrust, conflict between members, and conflict with the leader. At this point the leader's modeling is the leader's most important technique.

Create techniques to fit the context. In the working stage we see our principal role as following the material introduced by the members and opening these issues up for exploration rather than attempting to find solutions to problems. At this point we do not usually generate new issues; we try to follow the themes our clients give us, using techniques that facilitate the flow of topics and are adapted to them and that highlight connections between topics and links between members.

Provide opportunities to consolidate learning and to practice. We claim that the final stage of a group presents an ideal opportunity for using techniques that enable members to remember the specifics of their group experience, to reflect on and to seek a cognitive framework for lessons they want to take away, to practice new behavior, and to deal with the emotional significance of termination. This stage is important if the group is to be more than a passing experience; it should promote consolidation, generalization, and transfer of learning.

Learn to dance with clients. Our most general point is that group techniques cannot be an artificial substitute for a therapeutic and human encounter between you and the individuals who trust you to facilitate their group. Techniques can creatively enhance this encounter and give form to its expression, however, when you learn to dance with your clients.

Suggested Readings

Blatner, H. A. *Acting-in: Practical applications of psychodramatic methods.* New York: Springer, 1973. A useful guide for using psychodramatic techniques in groups, this brief book is written clearly and contains excellent discussions of the basic elements of psychodrama, its methods, stages, principles, and applications, as well as some of its pitfalls.

Branden, N. *The disowned self.* New York: Bantam Books, 1971. This book describes some therapeutic techniques, especially sentence-completion methods, to surface disowned feelings and thoughts.

Burnside, I. M. (Ed.). *Working with the elderly: Group processes and techniques.* North Scituate, Mass.: Duxbury, 1978. Those group leaders who are interested in getting practical hints on working with the elderly in groups will find this a most helpful resource.

Corey, G. *I never knew I had a choice.* Monterey, Calif.: Brooks/Cole, 1978. This book reviews many existential concerns and issues that clients bring to therapy such as those dealing with autonomy, work, love, sex, intimacy, loneliness, death, and meaning. The book discusses the bases on which we make choices for ourselves and how we shape our lives by the choices we make. It contains many exercises and activities that leaders can use for their group work and that they can suggest as homework assignments between sessions. Each chapter is followed by numerous annotated suggestions for further reading.

Corey, G. *Theory and practice of group counseling.* Monterey, Calif.: Brooks/Cole, 1981. This text surveys the key concepts and techniques that flow from the major theories of group counseling. It also discusses the stages of groups, group membership and group leadership, and ethical and professional issues in group practice. A student manual with exercises and techniques for small groups is also available.

Corey, G. *Case approach to counseling and psychotherapy.* Monterey, Calif.: Brooks/Cole, 1982. This book presents separate case studies along with ideas for techniques drawn from contemporary counseling approaches; the studies illustrate contrasting styles in working with the same client. The techniques described are also applicable to working with clients in groups.

Corey, G. *Theory and practice of counseling and psychotherapy* (2nd ed.). Monterey, Calif.: Brooks/Cole, 1982. This book describes eight models of therapy and counseling that are applicable to both individual and group therapy. It also discusses basic issues in counseling, ethical issues, and the counselor as a person. The book is designed to give the reader an overview of the theoretical basis of the practice of counseling. A student manual is available to assist readers in applying the concepts to their personal growth.

Corey, G., & Corey, M. S. *Groups: Process and practice.* Monterey, Calif.: Brooks/Cole, 1977. Much of this book deals with practical and professional issues specific to group work. Separate chapters are devoted to group leadership, ethical and professional issues, and applications of group procedures to populations of different ages.

Corey, G., Corey, M. S., & Callanan, P. J. *Professional and ethical issues in counseling and psychotherapy.* Monterey, Calif.: Brooks/Cole, 1979. A combination of textbook and student manual, this book contains self-inventories, open-ended cases, exercises, and suggested activities. It deals with a range of professional issues pertinent to group work.

Dinkmeyer, D. C., Pew, W. L., & Dinkmeyer, D. C., Jr. *Adlerian counseling and psychotherapy.* Monterey, Calif.: Brooks/Cole, 1979. This book is a clear and readable source with ideas for working with children, adults, adolescents, and families in groups. It contains concise descriptions of Adlerian techniques that can be used in groups.

Egan, G. *Interpersonal living: A skills/contract approach to human-relations training in groups.* Monterey, Calif.: Brooks/Cole, 1976. The author presents a contract approach to training in interpersonal skills. Chapters are devoted to self-disclosure, listening and responding, and challenging and confronting.

Ellis, A. *Humanistic psychotherapy: The rational-emotive approach.* New York: McGraw-Hill, 1973. This book gives a good overview of most of the basic concepts of the rational-emotive approach to psychotherapy. The chapters on self-awareness and personal growth of the therapist and the goals of psychotherapy are especially relevant to some of the topics explored in this book.

Feder, B., & Ronall, R. (Eds.). *Beyond the hot seat: Gestalt approaches to group.* New York: Brunner/Mazel, 1980. This book contains some informative articles on the process of Gestalt groups along with techniques to use with various populations. The book includes descriptions of art therapy in groups, movement therapy in groups, and marathons.

Frazen, J., & Shepherd, I. *Gestalt therapy now.* New York: Harper & Row, 1970. This book contains some excellent reading on the theory and techniques of Gestalt therapy, much of which is applicable to group work.

Gazda, G. (Ed.). *Basic approaches to group psychotherapy and group counseling.* Springfield, Ill.: Charles C Thomas, 1975. This survey text describes the theory and techniques related to the major group models.

Gazda, G. *Group counseling: A developmental approach* (2nd ed.). Boston: Allyn & Bacon, 1978. This is a basic book on group process with a developmental orientation and an emphasis on school counseling. It contains chapters on group procedures for preschoolers, young children, preadolescents, adolescents, and adults. It also covers group-counseling research and ethical and professional issues.

Glasser, W. *Reality therapy.* New York: Harper & Row, 1965. Outlining the basic concepts of reality therapy, Glasser shows how these principles apply to counseling people in institutions, particularly people with behavioral problems. This book deals with basic issues such as the place of values and morality in counseling, the counselor as a role model, the nature of reality, and therapy as a teaching/learning process.

Goldberg, C. *Therapeutic partnership: Ethical concerns in psychotherapy.* New York: Springer, 1977. This book presents an ethically enlightened approach to the practice of psychotherapy based on informed consent and psychological contract. It joins two major themes: the search for an understanding of human existence through therapeutic encounter and client/therapist collaborative endeavors in establishing a therapeutic partnership.

Goulding, M., & Goulding, R. *Changing lives through redecision therapy.* New York: Brunner/Mazel, 1979. This is an excellent book that gives ways to integrate Gestalt and transactional-analysis approaches and techniques in group work. Leaders can get many ideas they may want to experiment with in their groups.

Hansen, J. C., Warner, R. W., & Smith, E. M. *Group counseling: Theory and process* (2nd ed.). Chicago: Rand McNally, 1980. This survey text covers most of the contemporary models of group counseling and describes techniques and approaches that flow from these theories. It contains chapters on group membership, group leadership, and the stages in the life of a group.

Harper, R. *The new psychotherapies.* Englewood Cliffs, N. J.: Prentice-Hall, 1975. This is a good, although brief, overview of group therapies (including transactional analysis and encounter). It also deals with family therapies, the behavior therapies, and the body psychotherapies.

James, M., & Jongeward, D. *Born to win: Transactional analysis with Gestalt experiments.* Reading, Mass.: Addison-Wesley, 1971. An overview of the concepts of transactional analysis and descriptions of many Gestalt experiments make this book useful for group leaders.

Jourard, S. *Transparent self* (Rev. ed.). New York: Van Nostrand Reinhold, 1971. The author contends that our many ways of concealing ourselves lead to sickness and that openness is one way of increasing self-knowledge. The book contains excellent chapters on encounter groups and a way of being for group leaders.

Kopp, S. *If you meet the Buddha on the road, kill him!* New York: Bantam Books, 1976. This book not only describes what psychotherapy is like for patients but also stresses the involvement of the therapist in the process.

Laing, R. D. *The politics of experience.* New York: Pantheon, 1967. As a critic of traditional psychodiagnosis, Laing warns that a psychiatric label may become a self-fulfilling prophecy for both the client and the therapist. Labels influence the way hospital personnel view and treat patients, which in turn affects how patients view themselves and how they behave.

Lakin, M. *Interpersonal encounter: Theory and practice in sensitivity training.* New York: McGraw-Hill, 1972. Lakin explores professional issues related to training groups and encounter groups. The book covers policy issues, psychological risks, pregroup concerns, selection and recruitment, ethical questions, and evaluation.

Leveton, E. *Psychodrama for the timid clinician.* New York: Springer, 1977. The author offers an excellent view of psychodramatic techniques. Group leaders can benefit greatly from reading the book and following the author's advice to use experiential techniques in group work.

Lewis, H., & Streitfeld, H. *Growth games.* New York: Bantam Books, 1970. This is a cookbook of techniques based on the human potential movement. The authors catalog a wide range of games and techniques designed to sharpen one's senses, expand consciousness, develop breathing, achieve relaxation, and break through blocks.

Maslow, A. *Toward a psychology of being.* (2nd ed.). New York: Van Nostrand Reinhold, 1968. This book deals with issues such as growth and motivation, creativity, values, and the self-actualizing person.

Maslow, A. *Motivation and personality* (2nd ed.). New York: Harper & Row, 1970. The chapter on self-actualizing people provides a useful frame of reference for developing general goals for counseling and psychotherapy.

May, R. *Psychology and the human dilemma.* New York: Van Nostrand Reinhold, 1967. May describes the roots of contemporary problems of living such as the loss of significance and the anxiety of living in an anonymous world. May raises value issues that are relevant to psychotherapy, and he also discusses the social responsibilities of psychologists.

Mintz, E. *Marathon groups: Reality and symbol.* New York: Avon, 1971. This is an excellent book for either group leaders or members who desire to understand the dynamics of marathon groups. The book discusses the nature of marathons, the process of marathons, the uses of the past, and the group as therapist; and it gives suggestions for marathon leaders and describes techniques for enhancing awareness.

Mullan, H., & Rosenbaum, M. *Group psychotherapy: Theory and practice* (2nd ed.). New York: Free Press, 1978. A comprehensive treatment of groups from the psychoanalytic perspective with emphasis on techniques and procedures, the book focuses on methods to use from the beginning to the termination of analytically oriented groups.

Otto, H. *Group methods to actualize human potential—A handbook.* Beverly Hills, Calif.: Holistic Press, 1970. This catalog of group techniques for encounter and personal-growth groups offers many ideas for dealing with themes such as being a child and living one's fantasies.

Passons, W. R. *Gestalt approaches in counseling.* New York: Holt, Rinehart & Winston, 1975. This is a clear, concise, and practical account of the application of Gestalt principles to group counseling. It contains some extremely useful material on group techniques for centering in the present, expanding awareness, using verbal and nonverbal approaches, using fantasy, working with feelings, and dealing with the past and future.

Perls, F. *Gestalt therapy verbatim.* Lafayette, Calif.: Real People Press, 1969. Perls gives an informal, easy-to-read description of most of the basic concepts of Gestalt therapy. Of particular interest are discussions of the goals of therapy, responsibility, the client/therapist relationship, diagnosis, and the functions and roles of the therapist.

Polster, E., & Polster, M. *Gestalt therapy integrated.* New York: Random House,

1973. An excellent treatment of some advanced concepts underlying the practice of Gestalt therapy, this book describes clearly the nature of Gestalt therapy and emphasizes the role and function of the therapist. The authors point out that if therapists ignore using their personal qualities as an instrument in therapy they become mere technicians.

Rainwater, J. *You're in charge: A guide to becoming your own therapist.* Los Angeles: Guild of Tutors Press, 1979. This excellent self-help book provides leaders with ideas for using journals, autobiographies, and fantasy approaches in groups.

Rogers, C. *On becoming a person.* Boston: Houghton Mifflin, 1961. This important work describes the characteristics of the helping relationship from a person-centered viewpoint.

Rogers, C. *Carl Rogers on encounter groups.* New York: Harper & Row, 1970. This readable book on the process of the basic encounter group deals with how leaders can be facilitative in groups and what changes occur in people and in organizations as a result of participating in encounter groups.

Rose, S. D. *Group therapy: A behavioral approach.* Englewood Cliffs, N. J.: Prentice-Hall, 1977. This well-written book shows how to set up and conduct behavioral groups. It features descriptions of group techniques for various populations.

Rose S. D. (Ed.). *A casebook in group therapy: A behavioral-cognitive approach.* Englewood Cliffs, N. J.: Prentice-Hall, 1980. This reader contains contributions from 15 practicing behavior therapists. Among the topics covered are assertiveness training in groups, working with the elderly, prevention of obesity, working with school children, working with couples, and training groups.

Ruitenbeek, H. *The new group psychotherapies.* New York: Discus/Avon, 1970. This book provides a comprehensive overview of new approaches in group therapy, marathon groups, and styles of conducting encounter groups.

Schutz, W. *Joy: Expanding human awareness.* New York: Grove Press, 1967. The theme of this book is that joy is the result of realizing our full potential. Methods of enhancing personal functioning and interpersonal relating are the core of the book. This is a good book for persons thinking about becoming involved in a here-and-now group.

Schutz, W. *Here comes everybody.* New York: Harper & Row, 1971. This good treatment of the open encounter group is highly recommended for group leaders and participants who want to get an overview of various types of growth groups. Schutz discusses techniques and types of groups and has a good section on the group leader.

Shaffer, J., & Galinsky, M. D. *Models of group therapy and sensitivity training.* Englewood Cliffs, N. J.: Prentice-Hall, 1974. This book provides an excellent overview of the various models of groups including psychoanalytic, existential-experiential, psychodramatic, Gestalt, behavioristic, T-groups, encounter, and theme centered. The final chapter on integration and perspectives is excellent.

Shapiro, J. L. *Methods of group psychotherapy and encounter: A tradition of innovation.* Itasca, Ill.: Peacock, 1978. This is an excellent introductory text on group process with emphasis on the stages of groups and techniques appropriate for these stages. The author also deals with ethical and professional issues.

Szasz, T. *The myth of mental illness: Foundations of a theory of personal conduct.* New York: Delta, 1961. Szasz challenges the use of the medical model in psychotherapy. His thesis is that mental illness does not exist in the sense in which physical diseases do; and he challenges the idea that people should be excused for their behavior on the grounds that they are mentally ill and therefore not responsible for their acts.

Van Hoose, W., & Kottler, J. *Ethical and legal issues in counseling and psychotherapy.* San Francisco: Jossey-Bass, 1977. The authors deal with a variety of professional issues such as incompetent and unethical behavior, psychotherapy and the law, legal regulation of professional psychology, ethics in group work, marketing therapeutic services, behavior therapy, diagnosis and assessment, value problems, and ethical principles in the practice of therapy.

Yalom, I. *The theory and practice of group psychotherapy* (2nd ed.). New York: Basic Books, 1975. An excellent and comprehensive text on group therapy, this book presents detailed discussions of the curative factors in groups, the group therapist, procedures in organizing therapy groups, problem patients, research on encounter groups, and the training of group therapists.

Index

To the owner of this book:

We enjoyed writing this book, and it is our hope that you have enjoyed reading it. We'd like to know about your experiences with the book; only through your comments and the comments of others can we assess the impact of this book and make it a better book for readers in the future.

School: _____

Instructor's name: _____

1. What did you like *most* about the book? _____
_____

_____

2. What did you like *least* about the book? _____
_____

3. How useful were the *questions and activities* at the end of the chapters?
_____

_____

4. What class did you use this book for? _____

5. In the space below or in a separate letter, please tell us what it was like for you to read this book and how you used it; please give your suggestions for revisions and any other comments you'd like to make about the book; include if you'd like your own ideas for group techniques.

Optional:

Your name: _____ Date: _____

May Brooks/Cole quote you, either in promotion for *Group Techniques* or in future publishing ventures?

Yes _____ No _____

Sincerely,

Gerald Corey
Marianne Schneider Corey
Patrick J. Callanan
J. Michael Russell

FOLD HERE

NO POSTAGE
NECESSARY
IF MAILED
IN THE
UNITED STATES

BUSINESS REPLY MAIL
FIRST CLASS   PERMIT NO. 84   MONTEREY, CALIF.

POSTAGE WILL BE PAID BY ADDRESSEE

COREY/COREY/CALLANAN/RUSSELL
BROOKS/COLE PUBLISHING CO.
MONTEREY, CA 93940-3286